$\mathcal{E}$ndless Love . . .

"Everyone wants love. We dream about it, fantasize about a perfect partner, and visualize finding a lasting relationship. Yet, in real life, the right partner can seem endlessly elusive. I believe that there is a special person for everyone. The perfect person for you is either already with you, or is searching for you. The hard part is finding that special person. However, you *can* do it. The two of you have been together countless times before. You may have enjoyed a passionate romance in ancient Egypt, medieval England, or Renaissance Rome. You may have spent pleasant lifetimes in the Holy Land, Thailand, or Russia. You found your soul mate then. You can do it again in this lifetime. The purpose of this book is to help you find—and then keep—this special person."

About the Author

Richard Webster was born in New Zealand in 1946, where he still resides. He travels widely every year, lecturing and conducting workshops on psychic subjects around the world. He has written many books, mainly on psychic subjects, and also writes monthly magazine columns. Richard is married with three children. His family is very supportive of his occupation, but his oldest son, after watching his father's career, has decided to become an accountant.

Other Books by Richard Webster

Astral Travel for Beginners

Aura Reading for Beginners

Dowsing for Beginners

Feng Shui for Beginners

Llewellyn Feng Shui series

Numerology Magic

Omens, Oghams & Oracles

101 Feng Shui Tips for the Home

Palm Reading for Beginners

Seven Secrets to Success

Spirit Guides and Angel Guardians

Forthcoming

Success Secrets: Letters to Matthew

Many of Llewellyn's authors have websites with additional information and resources. For more information, please visit our website at www.llewellyn.com.

Understanding Relationships Across Time

Soul
Mates

Richard Webster

2001
Llewellyn Publications
St. Paul, Minnesota 55164-0383, U.S.A.

First Edition
First Printing, 2001

Book design and editing by Michael Maupin
Cover design by Anne-Marie Garrison

Library of Congress Cataloging-in-Publication Data
Webster, Richard, 1946–
    Soul mates : understanding relationships across time / Richard
        Webster.—1st ed.
        p.   cm.
    Includes bibliographical references and index.
    ISBN 1-56718-789-7
    1. Soul mates. I. Title.

BF1045.I58 W43 2001
133.9—dc21   00-051448

Llewellyn Worldwide does not participate in, endorse, or have any authority or responsibility concerning private business transactions between our authors and the public.
    All mail addressed to the author is forwarded but the publisher cannot, unless specifically instructed by the author, give out an address or phone number.

Llewellyn Publications
A Division of Llewellyn Worldwide, Ltd.
P.O. Box 64383, Dept. 1-56718-789-7
St. Paul, MN 55164-0383, U.S.A.
www.llewellyn.com

Printed in the United States of America

For Margaret

My Soul Mate

Contents

Introduction

What is mind? No matter. What is matter?
Never mind. What is the soul? It is immaterial.

—Thomas Hood

IN 1967, at the ripe age of twenty, I worked my passage from New Zealand to London on a ship. I arrived one evening, and the next morning began exploring the West End. To my surprise, I encountered friends from New Zealand. They were going to a party that night, and suggested that I join them. It was a good party, mainly because I made a friend there—Margaret Shaw. Four years later we married. I had travelled to England to progress in my career in publishing. Nothing could have been further from my mind at the time than finding a life partner. Yet, a particular set of circumstances brought us together. If I had not bumped into my friends, or had chosen not to go to the party, I would not have met Margaret. If she had not happened to be good friends with the people who were hosting the party, she would not have been there either. Was our meeting pure chance, or was it predestined?

As soon as Margaret and I became a couple, friends began telling us, "You're obviously soul mates." However, this was swinging London in the 1960s, and many people were talking freely about soul mates. Consequently, I paid little attention to their comments.

However, every now and again over the years, in my work as a hypnotherapist, couples would come to me wanting past-life regressions to see if they had been together in previous lifetimes. I enjoy conducting regressions, and find it fascinating to see how couples have been inextricably entwined over many generations. The relationships and sexes change, but the person being hypnotized can instantly recognize his or her soul mate in these past-life regressions.

Unfortunately, though, it did not always work. Some couples came to me convinced that they were soul mates and had been together in previous lifetimes. However, although they entered hypnosis easily and regressed back to different past lives, their partner in this lifetime was not there. Did this mean that they were not soul mates after all?

I have also experienced the opposite scenario where my subjects were convinced that their partner in this lifetime was not a soul mate. Yet, when they were regressed their partners figured in every one.

Consequently, I had the situation where some people were convinced that they were soul mates, and hypnotic regressions confirmed this. Other people also thought they were soul mates, but we were unable to verify this. And yet other people thought they were not soul mates, but past-life regressions indicated that they were.

This was confusing, to say the least. I began reading everything I could find on the subject, and asked questions everywhere I went. The interest in soul mates was enormous. It seemed that everyone was in search of their personal soul mate. Everyone had a secret wish to find that perfect someone with whom they had shared many, many previous incarnations.

I found that people had different ideas about what a soul mate was. Many people thought that it simply meant a special, unusually close relationship where each partner lived purely for the other. Others described it as a relationship where the couple were friends as well as lovers. Most people defined it as a strong love attachment between a man and a woman that lasted over many lifetimes.

My own definition is that a soul mate relationship is a strong bond between two people that has existed over many incarnations, where each partner helps the other to learn the lessons that he or she needs to learn in this incarnation.

I believe that soul mates are not restricted to heterosexual relationships, and can be between two people of the same sex. They are not necessarily love relationships, either. I also believe that soul mate relationships do not necessarily last for a whole lifetime. A few years ago, good friends of ours divorced after fifteen years of marriage. I was amazed at the time, as I considered them to be soul mates. I still believe that, but feel that they had learned the lessons that they needed to learn from each other, and consequently, were now moving on.

People have believed in soul mates for thousands of years. Plato wrote in his *Symposium* that humans had been looking for their soul mate ever since Zeus had cut them in half. In his mythic story, Plato describes a world where there were men, women, and people who were both men and women. Apparently, humans began discussing how they could climb up to heaven and replace the gods. The gods were upset by this and discussed what should be done. The simplest solution would be to destroy mankind, but Zeus came up with a better idea. He suggested cutting all human beings in half. This would serve two purposes. First, it would immediately double the number of people making offerings to the gods. Second, it would weaken the humans, so they would not be able to carry out their plan.

Zeus' idea was accepted, and the humans were all divided into two. Naturally, the humans were upset at this, and Zeus decided to enable each half to have intercourse with their opposite, symbolically creating a whole. Consequently, the males sought other males, the females other females, and the people who had been both male and female sought their other half, allowing the population to reproduce.[1] Plato's account is an interesting story, and shows that belief in soul mates is extremely old. In fact, his idea of somehow dividing a "whole" person in half dates back even further. In the Bible we are told that God created a being that was "in his own image" (Genesis 1:27). From this perfect being, God took a rib and created a woman (Genesis 2:21–23). Consequently, Adam and Eve must have been soul mates.

In Ra mythology, in the Egyptian tradition, the gods Isis and Osiris were soul mates. This 5,000-year-old story tells how Isis and Osiris were twins, who began life together in the womb. It was even believed that they had intercourse together while still in the womb.[2] They grew up and married. Their love for each other was so great that even death could not separate them. Osiris was killed by his jealous brother Set, who desired both Isis and the kingdom. The coffin containing Osiris was dumped in the Nile and floated to Byblos. Isis found it and brought it back to Egypt. This infuriated Set who divided Osiris' dead body into fourteen pieces and scattered them throughout the country. Isis managed to find all the pieces, except for the penis, which had been eaten by the Oxyrhyncus crab. She made a penis out of clay, and then transformed herself into a vulture. She brought the corpse of Osiris back to life by flapping her wings, and they made passionate love together. Their son, Horus, was the result of this strange sexual union.

This fascinating story had enormous appeal to the ancient Egyptians and made Osiris one of their most popular gods. It demonstrated how Osiris had transcended death and achieved immortality. This, for the first time, gave people hope that they also could become immortal. It demonstrated the powerful love of a man and a woman, and how that love can continue to grow even after the death of one partner. Not surprisingly, Abydos, the place where Osiris was believed to have been buried, became one of the most sacred sites in Egypt.[3]

The story also started a tradition in which the king was named Horus, but became Osiris after his physical death. His successor was then named Horus in turn, thus ensuring the divinity of the king.

Love has been the topic of wonderful stories ever since people began communicating with each other. No other word means as much as the simple word "love." Many people read books and watch movies simply to recapture the feelings of a couple falling in love and, hopefully, living happily ever after. Everyone wants love. We dream about it, fantasize about a perfect partner, and visualize finding a lasting relationship. Yet, in real life, the right partner can seem endlessly elusive. I believe that there is a special person for everyone. The perfect person for you is either already with you, or is searching for you. The hard part is finding that special person. However, you can do it. The two of you have been together countless times before. You may have enjoyed a passionate romance in ancient Egypt, medieval England, or Renaissance Rome. You may have spent pleasant lifetimes in the Holy Land, Thailand, or Russia. You found your soul mate then. You can do it again in this lifetime. The purpose of this book is to help you find—and then keep—this special person. I want you to find your soul mate, and enjoy a lifelong relationship with him or her.

Soul Mates

Our birth is but a sleep and a forgetting;
The Soul that rises with us, our Life's Star,
Hath had elsewhere its setting,
And cometh from afar.

—William Wordsworth, "Ode:
Intimations of Immortality"

Before we can start talking about soul mates, we need to find out what a soul is. Most dictionaries define it as the spiritual part of a human being, and some go further and say that it may be immortal. In fact, it is all of this, and more. The soul is responsible for all of the higher aspects of life that make us human. Without the soul, we would not be able to express or experience love. All of the noblest activities of life are due to the soul. The soul also represents the living aspect of the body. When the soul leaves, the body dies. Consequently, the soul is also responsible for all of our bodily functions and could be considered synonymous with the mind or spirit. However, it is much more than all that. It represents life itself, and if the soul is immortal, we can not die. We simply move into another sphere of existence. Our soul existed before we entered this lifetime, and will continue to exist after we leave it. John Bradshaw says that the soul "reveals the depth and mystery of beings."[1]

William Faulkner, the American novelist, gave his definition of the soul in his Nobel Prize speech. He said: "I believe man will not merely endure, he will prevail. He is immortal, not because he, alone among creatures, has an inexhaustible voice but because he has a soul, a spirit capable of compassion and sacrifice and endurance."[2]

Many years ago I knew a woman who was petrified of accidentally losing her soul. She had heard that it was possible for this to happen whenever she yawned or sneezed. Consequently, whenever she sneezed, she always said, "God bless me," to ensure that her soul did not escape. Naturally, she also said, "God bless," whenever anyone else sneezed in her presence. This lady also tried to stifle her yawns, and would completely cover her mouth to prevent the soul from escaping whenever she needed to yawn. I never told her that some races of people believe that the soul can escape during sleep.[3]

It is fortunate that the work of Thomas Moore, Michael Newton, and others has returned the word "soul" to our vocabulary. During the last century the idea of a soul was gradually being forgotten. This was one of the factors of modern life that concerned Carl Jung.[4]

However, the word "soul" is gradually coming back into our vocabulary. We have always had expressions such as "soulful," "lost souls," "old souls," and "the eyes are the windows of the soul." Today we can add terms such as "soul food" and "soul music" to the list.

In his book *The Man Who Can Look Backward,* Noel Street talks about a gynecologist friend of his who loves looking into the eyes of babies after birth. He found that by doing this he can discern new souls from the old. Some babies eyes were filled with a "look of apprehension and fear," while others looked around much "more casually as if appraising their 'new' situation." The gynecologist said that "it was as if they were saying: 'Now what—this time?'"[5] Eyes truly are the windows of the soul.

If we accept the definition of soul mates as being a strong bond between two people that has existed through many incarnations, we also need to accept the idea of reincarnation.

Reincarnation is the doctrine that says that we evolve spiritually by living as many lifetimes as is necessary to achieve perfection. In other words, although our physical body and personality die, our soul is immortal. It has already experienced many lifetimes and has many more yet to come. When we are born our soul brings with it all the knowledge, experience, wisdom, and karma we have gained from previous lifetimes. Consequently, the qualities we express are the result of our long lineage of previous lifetimes. What we learn in this lifetime will also be added to this record for use in future lifetimes. The way we live in this lifetime has a direct effect on the quality of life we will experience in our next incarnation.

Reincarnation is an extremely old concept that has given comfort to countless people over the years.[6] It has been part of the teachings of many religions, including Judaism and Christianity. Today it is probably more popular than ever, with at least half of the world's population accepting it as fact. Acceptance of reincarnation has been steadily increasing in the United States. In 1969, a Gallup poll discovered that almost 20 percent of Americans believed in life after death. The same survey in 1981, showed that 23 percent of Americans believed in reincarnation.[7] By 1994, a Gallup poll found that the number of Americans who believed in reincarnation had increased to 27 percent.[8]

The reason why so many people believe in reincarnation is that throughout history, countless people have had memories of their past lives. A few have entered into their current lives with strong memories of their most recent past lives, and frequently this information has been able to be verified. Dr. Ian Stevenson is the world's leading expert on people who have conscious memories of their past lives. Now in his eighties, he has spent most of his life researching this subject and investigating the claims of people who recall their past lives.[9] However, only a comparatively small number of people consciously recall their past lives. This does not mean that most people have not lived before, as hypnotic regressions show that virtually everyone is able to return to not just one, but many, previous lifetimes.

One of the arguments against reincarnation is that there are more people alive now than at any other time in the history of the planet. The population of the world doubled between the first century C.E. and 1500. It doubled again between then and the nineteenth century, and has since increased four times. Where are all these souls coming from? It is possible that new souls are being created all the time. However, a more likely explanation is that people are being reincarnated more quickly nowadays than ever before. In fact, once you die, the chances are that you will be born again in approximately fifty-two years.[10]

Helen Wambach has done extensive research on this subject. She found that her clients reflected historical reality to a remarkable extent. For instance, her clients returned to different periods of history in exact proportion to that which represented the world's population at the time. She also found that with all of her regressions the ratio between male and female was almost exactly equal, even though the proportion of male and female clients she regressed varied greatly.

It is a common misconception that people who are regressed choose to become famous historical figures. I have not found this to be the case myself, and Helen Wambach found exactly the same. People who are regressed do not usually live glamorous, rich, and successful lives. One of Helen Wambach's clients regressed to a past life in Pakistan where he was a cripple. He became a beggar and died of starvation. Another one was a barmaid in England who died after she was raped and beaten by several drunken men. No one would ever deliberately choose these lives when undertaking a past-life regression.

Helen Wambach classified the results she obtained over a four thousand year period. She was able to ask questions that enabled her to classify her clients as being upper, middle, or lower class in each period. Upper class lives were always a small minority, and most people led lower class lives. This again conforms with the reality of the different time frames she was examining.[11]

Reincarnation is a satisfying concept on many levels. It helps explain karma. This is the law of cause and effect. We ultimately receive what we give. As the Bible says: "Whatsoever a man soweth, that shall he also reap" (Galatians 6:7). We create our own karma by the way in which we lead our lives. If we do a good deed today, we will eventually be rewarded, though not necessarily in this lifetime. Likewise, if we do harm, we will eventually be punished. If we are rich but lazy in this lifetime, at some stage we will have to work hard and struggle to make ends meet to balance out this experience.

Karma allows us freedom of choice. It is fair and automatic. It has nothing to do with morality, and there is no sense of judgment in it. There is a great deal of injustice in the world, but the law of karma ultimately takes care of it and balances the books. Plato described this well when he wrote: "Virtue has no master, and as a man honors or despises her, so will he have more of her or less. The responsibility is on him that chooseth. There is none on God."[12]

Karma also affects our personalities. As we are here to learn certain lessons, we are given certain physical, mental, emotional, psychological, and spiritual qualities at birth, and these shape our entire lives. Seeing reality through these qualities allows us to experience the various situations that will help our growth and development. Of course, in this lifetime, we are not just paying off karmic debts. Through the experiences of our lives, and our reactions to them, we also pick up karmic debts that will have to be paid back later, either in this lifetime or in a future life. We will also gain karmic credits for our good deeds.

It is not what happens to us that is important, it is how we react to them. If we respond to a negative situation in a positive way, we are effectively creating good karma, rather than bad. It means that we have learned the lesson and can move on. Conversely, if we react to the situation in a negative way, by becoming angry, stressed out, bitter, jealous, and full of desires for revenge, it shows that we have not learned the lesson. As a result, at some stage, we will be presented with a similar situation again. This will continue to happen until we finally learn the lesson. I have found many people who have experienced virtually identical situations in several previous lifetimes. Obviously, the lesson was being repeated over and over again until, finally, the soul learned it and was able to move forwards again.

At one time I owned a bookstore. Several years after selling it, I received a small check in the post from someone who had stolen a book from my store. An anonymous letter came with the check, apologizing for what he or she had done, and expressing the hope that this action would pay off the karmic debt that had been created by stealing the book. Fortunately, this person was aware of what he or she had done, and had made amends. Many people shoplift and give it no further thought. They experience no guilt at the time, and are totally unaware that they are creating karmic debts for themselves.

Not everyone likes the idea of coming back again and again. I couldn't begin to calculate the number of times people have said to me, "I don't want to come back. Once is enough for me." I have to tell these people that they will not be coming back as themselves. The person they are now will ultimately die, and their present personality will disappear. However, their soul is immortal and will ultimately be given a new identity. Consequently, when two people are attracted to each other and feel that they are "soul mates," it is truly the souls that were "mates" in previous lifetimes.

If we have already experienced countless previous lives, why can we not remember them? It is probably extremely fortunate that we do not. Forgetfulness is not always a bad thing. Imagine the complications that would be created if we were trying to live one life, while full of memories of another. Even in our current lives we usually have no memory of learning essential skills, such as walking and talking. It appears also that oxytocin, a hormone produced by the mother's posterior pituitary gland, bathes the unborn child in the latter stages of pregnancy. Oxytocin causes memory loss in laboratory animals, and might explain why we can not remember our past lives.[13]

Consequently, it is unusual for soul mates to recall any of the intimate details of their previous lifetimes together. This is not surprising, as their current personalities have no conscious memories of their past lives. It is the soul that remembers. However, their hearts open wide when they first meet in this lifetime and an immediate attraction is felt. Each incarnation strengthens and deepens the relationship, until finally they reach a state of total, perfect love.

I am often told that a belief in reincarnation goes against the tenets of Christianity. The Council of Constantinople in 553 C.E. condemned Origen's teachings on the pre-existence of the soul. Anyone who taught Origen's ideas was declared anathema (excommunicated, or banned by the church).[14] However, it appears from the Bible that reincarnation was commonly accepted. In the Gospel According to Matthew (16:13–14) we read:

> When Jesus came into the coasts of Caesarea Philippi, he asked his disciples, saying, Whom do men say that I the Son of man am? And they said, Some say that thou art John the Baptist; some Elias; and others, Jeremias, or one of the prophets.

In John 9:34 the disciples asked Jesus about a man who had been born blind, thinking that he was being punished for a sin. "Which did sin, this man or his parents?" they asked. Obviously, the disciples were thinking of reincarnation, as the man was born blind and any sin must have occurred in a previous lifetime.

In the Apocrypha we find: "Now I was a child good by nature, and a good soul fell to my lot. Nay, rather being good, I came into a body undefiled" (The Wisdom of Solomon, 8:19–20).

Many Christian sects over the years have believed in reincarnation. These include the Cathars, the Paulicians, and Bogomils.[15] However, they were invariably castigated and punished by the church establishment. Giordano Bruno (1548–1600), a leading philosopher, scientist, and poet of the Renaissance, was burned at the stake because he believed in reincarnation.[16]

Other religions were more open in their acceptance of reincarnation. For instance, in the Koran we read: "God generates beings, and sends them back over and over again, till they return to Him."

In China they have a saying which encompasses both reincarnation and soul mates. "It takes ten years of hard work in a past life to create the necessary fate to enable you to cross a river in the same boat as someone. It then takes a further hundred years of work to enable the two of you to share the same pillow."

According to Chinese legend, our fates regarding marriage partners are determined by the Old Man Under the Moon, who uses red thread to link the feet of boys and girls who are destined to become marriage partners. This ensures that they will ultimately meet. This explains the popular saying: "Those whom fate binds together will find each other though separated by a thousand *li*."[17]

Pythagoras and his school taught the principles of reincarnation, and throughout history many eminent people have believed in the concept of rebirth. These ideas have also appeared in the works of many poets including, Goethe, Milton, Shakespeare, Coleridge, Poe, Longfellow, Whitman, Shelley, Southey, Wordsworth, Browning, Blake, Yeats, and Masefield. Benjamin Franklin's famous epitaph for himself, written when he was only twenty-two, reveals his interest in the subject:

The Body of B. Franklin,
Printer,
Like the Cover of an Old Book,
Its Contents Torn Out
And
Stripped of its Lettering and Gilding,
Lies Here
Food for Worms,
But the Work shall not be Lost,
For it Will as He Believed
Appear Once More
In a New and more Elegant Edition
Revised and Corrected
By the Author.

Stories about soul mates have also proven fruitful to writers of fiction.

William Shakespeare is an excellent example of a writer who was well aware of the power that a strong love story has on an audience. Romeo and Juliet are obviously soul mates, and their tragic love affair has been reenacted countless times since it was first performed in 1594 or 1595. Twelve years later, he used the story of two real-life soul mates when he wrote *Antony and Cleopatra.*

Romeo and Juliet are invariably the first two names that spring to mind whenever the subject of soul mates comes up. Shakespeare, in his own life, made mistakes when it came to love. His own experiences may explain why so many of his characters find themselves under pressure to marry and satisfy other people's expectations. In *Romeo and Juliet*, Juliet is betrothed to Count Paris. If she marries him, she will lead a life of comfort and ease. Both pairs of parents will be happy, and everything would be perfect. However, she does not love him. When she meets Romeo, she instantly falls in love. However, he is a Montague and she is a Capulet. Such a love is impossible. However, Juliet is a strong woman and follows her heart. This was a difficult and dangerous thing to do in those days. After Romeo kills someone in a fight, the young lovers run away together. But the flight is doomed, and the story moves inexorably to its tragic end. As Shakespeare wrote in the final two lines of the play:

> For never was a story of more woe,
> Than this of Juliet and her Romeo.

In Act Two, Scene Two there is an indication that Shakespeare considered this tragic pair to be soul mates. Romeo says, after hearing Juliet call his name:

> It is my soul that calls upon my name:
> How silver-sweet sound lovers' tongues
>   by night,
> Like softest music to attending ears!

Shakespeare's plays show his remarkable insight into the nature of the soul, and the word "soul" appears many times in his works. Here are a few examples:

> Thou art a soul in bliss, but I am bound
> Upon a wheel of fire, that mine own tears
> Do scald like molten lead. *(King Lear)*

> Every subject's duty is the king's; but every subject's soul is his own. *(Henry V)*

> Lie down, and stray no further.
> Now all labour
> Mars what it does; yea, very force entangles
> Itself with strength. . . .
> Stay for me:
> Where souls do couch on flowers,
> we'll hand in hand,
> And with our sprightly port
> make the ghosts gaze;
> Dido and her Aeneas shall want troops,
> And all the haunt be ours.
> *(Antony and Cleopatra)*

> An oath, an oath, I have an oath in heaven;
> Shall I lay perjury upon my soul?
> No, not for Venice. *(The Merchant of Venice)*

> Sit, Jessica, look, how the floor of heaven
> Is thick inlaid with patines of bright gold;
> There's not the smallest orb
> which thou behold'st
> But in this motion like an angel sings

Still quiring to the young-eyed cherubins;
Such harmony is in immortal souls.
(*The Merchant of Venice*)

Although there are innumerable books about the passion and love two people feel for each other, not much has been written in fiction about the love between soul mates.

A notable exception is *The Three Gentlemen* by A. E. W. Mason (1865–1948), which describes three lifetimes a man and a woman shared over two thousand years.

The first lifetime is in Roman times. Attilius Scaurus is a young Roman from a good family who is sent to join the army in Britain after getting heavily in debt. He meets Sergia, the beautiful daughter of a wealthy Briton. When his regiment is called back to Rome he tries to contact Sergia, but is captured by her father's servants and eventually killed.

In the second lifetime, the hero is Anthony Scarr, who falls in love with Sylvia, the sister of a wealthy friend. Queen Elizabeth I comes to stay with his friends, and during the course of the weekend, Anthony disgraces and embarrasses himself and Sylvia in front of the queen. Sir Francis Walsingham, the queen's spymaster, had been watching Anthony for some time, and suggests that he work for him overseas for a time. Anthony plays a major role in England's success over the Spanish Armada, but is captured and hanged.

In his third lifetime, in the twentieth century, he is Adrian Shard, and falls in love with the step-daughter of a cabinet minister, Sonia. Adrian becomes the minister's private secretary and gradually discovers that there is much wrongdoing going on behind the scenes. The minister and his wife are opposed to the match, because they have arranged for Sonia to marry a financier of dubious reputation. The minister and the financier plot to have Adrian blamed for their wrongdoings, but Adrian outwits them and finally marries his soul mate, almost two thousand years after first meeting her.

An interesting aspect of this book is the way in which the characters gradually recall pivotal incidents from their previous incarnations, making this a true soul mate novel.

The Reincarnation Library have recently republished this book, as well as another soul mate novel called *Many, Many Times* by James Riddell. This book describes a passionate affair an engaged man has with his soul mate.[18] *After Death* by Ivan Turgenev also has a soul mate theme.

One book that almost qualifies as a soul mate book is the novel *Peter Ibbetson* by George du Maurier (1834–1896).[19] He was born in Paris and became an artist and book illustrator. His career as a writer began when he joined the staff of *Punch* magazine and wrote a regular column that gently satirized upper-class life. His most famous work is *Trilby,* which was published in 1894 and is still in print. *Peter Ibbetson* was published in 1891, and his final book, *The Martian*, was published after his death in 1896.

Peter Ibbetson begins with a small boy and girl playing together in the streets of Paris. Unfortunately, the boy's parents die and he is taken to London where he is brought up by a distant uncle. He adopts his uncle's surname, and gradually forgets about his childhood in Paris.

Many years later, he sees a beautiful woman at a party and is captivated by her. Someone tells him that she is the "Duchess of Towers." Although he does not speak to her, he cannot get her out of his mind.

Some time later, Peter returns to Paris and visits the neighborhood where he spent his early years. To his amazement, the Duchess of Towers passes him in a carriage.

That night he dreams of her, and the dream is more vivid than anything he has experienced before. He returns to London entirely transformed. Every night he has the most incredible dreams about the two of them together, and when he wakes up he can recall every detail.

Peter is invited to a dinner party, and the Duchess of Towers is also present. He asks the person beside him about her and discovers, with a shock, that she was the small girl he used to play with when he was young. He cannot believe that he failed to recognize her.

The following morning he meets the countess again, and explains who he was. She almost faints, as she has been experiencing the identical dreams that Peter has. The countess insists that they part, never to meet again.

Peter is devastated. Somehow he can no longer communicate with her in his dreams. He has a miserable year, which culminates when he argues with his uncle and accidentally kills him.

He is convicted of murder and sentenced to life imprisonment. Peter has a desperate need to explain what had happened to the Duchess of Towers. He starts to write her a letter, but falls asleep. The duchess appears to him in a dream and promises to write him a letter. This letter arrives the following morning. From that time on they continue to meet every night in their dreams. Although they gradually got old, in their dreams they were always young.

Finally, the countess dies. Peter tries to starve himself to death, but is unsuccessful. One night, in his dreams he returns to his childhood home in Paris. He is no longer young in this dream, and drags himself around. Finally, he finds himself at a beach, and sitting on the sand waiting for him is the countess.

She explains that she has returned with enormous difficulty to tell him that they are inseparable, and that death is not the end. They will be together for eternity.

This is an extremely brief précis of a remarkable work. Unfortunately, *Peter Ibbetson* is not currently in print, but there have been many editions of it over the years and it is readily available at secondhand book stores. It is well worth tracking down. The story of *Peter Ibbetson* has had a further two incarnations over the years. In 1915 a dramatized version became an extremely successful play, with productions in both London and New York, and in 1931 Deems Taylor's operatic version was performed by the Metropolitan Opera Company.

There are many short stories, from many different cultures, that tell of two lovers who cannot be separated even by death. The classic story of Isis and Osiris is a good example. Belief in reincarnation goes back to prehistoric times, and it is not hard to visualize people thousands of years ago listening entranced as a storyteller wove an exciting story about two soul mates.

The theme of reincarnation has always been a popular theme in literature. Jack London's novels *Before Adam* and *The Star Rover* are excellent examples, as is *I Live Again* by Warwick Deeping. H. Rider Haggard was a firm believer in reincarnation and remembered lives in Norway, Africa, and Egypt. His classic novel *She* contains a character who remembers her past lives.

The Nazarene by Sholem Asch concerns the life and crucifixion of Jesus. An elderly Polish man employs a young Jew to help him translate an ancient Hebrew document. He confides in the young man that he can remember a previous lifetime in Jerusalem when he was a Roman official who was involved in the crucifixion of Jesus. The young man records his story, and, as he does, gains recall of a previous life that he spent in Jerusalem at the time of Jesus. He writes his memories down, as well. The scroll they are translating turns out to be Judas Iscariot's account of the Gospel story. Consequently, the book contains three different accounts of the story of Jesus. Not surprisingly, this book was a bestseller when it appeared in 1939.

Bunker Bean by Harry Leon Wilson is one of my favorite books. It can be read on a number of levels: as a humorous novel, as a motivational book, and as a reincarnation novel. Bunker Bean was a timid, quiet man who was told by a fortuneteller that he was the reincarnation of Napoleon Bonaparte and an Egyptian king. He could not believe that he, a total failure in this life, had ruled over large parts of the world in the past. He read as much as he could about Napoleon and modeled himself on the man he used to be. He transformed himself and ended up as a captain of industry. He then discovered that the fortuneteller was a fraud, but the discovery came too late, as Bunker Bean was by now a highly successful person.[20]

Mark Twain's true story, "My Platonic Sweetheart," may well be about a soul mate. It recounts a recurring dream that Mark Twain experienced over a period of forty years about a fifteen-year-old girl with whom he shared a deep and innocent love.

The theme of reincarnation even appears in music. Richard Wagner strongly believed in reincarnation, and *The Flying Dutchman* could be described as a gripping story of reincarnation. The *Flying Dutchman* was a phantom ship. A murder took place on board, and since then the ship has haunted the sea, forever trying to reach Table Bay. Captain Frederick Marryat wrote a novel about this legend, called *The Phantom Ship* (1839). At one time Richard Wagner began an opera based on the theme of reincarnation called *Die Sieger (The Victor)*. However, he never finished it and ultimately used some of the music in *Parsifal*.[21]

There have also been many plays and short stories with a reincarnation theme. J. B. Priestley's *I Have Been Here Before* was a popular play that achieved critical acclaim as well. J. D. Salinger wrote a remarkable short story called "Teddy," about a ten-year-old American boy who could remember his past life as a Hindu yogi.[22]

Reincarnation has been a popular topic for movies and television, as well. The musical play, *On a Clear Day You Can See Forever* became a movie. *Switch* and *Goodbye, Charlie* are other examples. *My Mother the Car* depicted a woman who became rein-"car"-nated. *One Step Beyond* and *The X-Files* show the perennial interest in topics such as reincarnation.

Everyone has a soul. For thousands of years different religions have taught that the soul is immortal. The ancient Greeks had a dualistic view of the universe, dividing it into matter and spirit. They believed that Matter was ephemeral and dies, but Spirit was eternal. Consequently, human beings, made of Matter, naturally die, but the immortal soul, being Spirit, is immortal.

In *The Republic,* Plato argues that the soul is eternal. He asks his friend, Glaucon, if good preserves and benefits, and evil destroys and corrupts. Glaucon naturally agrees. Plato then asks him if evil harms and ultimately destroys anything it settles on. He uses illness and the human body as an example. Glaucon agrees again. Plato then asks him if the soul has any qualities that could make it evil. Glaucon says that it has, and suggests injustice, licentiousness, cowardice, and ignorance as examples. Plato then asks him if any of these things can destroy or dissolve the soul. Glaucon has to admit that they cannot.

Plato continues: "Then, when there is no one evil, whether belonging to itself or another, which destroys the soul, it must obviously exist for always, and, if it exists always, be immortal."[23]

The Greek belief in the immortality of the soul was ably demonstrated in the calm way in which Socrates approached his death. Like Plato, he believed that the soul was imprisoned in the body, and death set it free. Consequently, he drank the hemlock convinced that he was going to live with the gods in a much better existence than life here on earth.

As souls are immortal, they live outside time. Your soul has already lived and worked within the many different personalities and bodies of all the people who preceded you. Your soul has learned, grown, and evolved with each incarnation. In this current lifetime it is continuing to evolve, and how you choose to live your life plays a major part in the progress your soul can make. A wholly evil person is someone whose personality is unable to connect with his or her soul. This naturally slows down the evolvement of the soul. A truly good person has a personality that is in harmony with his or her soul. It is impossible to see where one ends and the other begins.

Our personality gives us our good and bad qualities and emotions, but it is the soul that gives us compassion and love. Consequently, soul mates love at a deep soul level that far transcends the love between two individuals who are not soul mates.

This even applies in nonromantic soul mate relationships. Soul mates are brought together to work on a specific task. A love relationship is what comes to most people's minds when they think of soul mates, but the variety of possible tasks is limitless. It might be to pay off a karmic debt or to work on a challenging project that both people consider worthwhile. The relationship may last only for the length of time necessary to complete the task, but the strong love bond will be apparent to others, even if it is not recognized by the people concerned.

Many years ago, a man came to me for hypnotherapy because he was concerned that he might be developing homosexual tendencies. He, and an older man, were composing an opera together. Consequently, they were spending a great deal of time in each other's company working on this project. They both felt passionate about the opera, and thought about little else. It is not surprising that this young man felt that he was falling in love with his partner, as they were spending all their time together working on something they considered of paramount importance.

In fact, although he did not know it, this young man had met one of his soul mates. Obviously, this was not a romantic union, but was a valid soul mate experience in which two people were working together on something important. Once the opera was completed, and had been performed, the two men went their separate ways. However, they had both grown enormously as a result of their time together.

Most people believe that they have a soul, but not everyone can accept that their soul has already experienced countless previous lifetimes. This is because the memory of previous lifetimes is stored at the soul level, and we need to make contact with this to recall our past experiences. There are a number of methods that can be used to discover your previous lives. For most people, the easiest way to do this is to experience a past-life regression. We will look at this in the next chapter.

Past-Life Regression

I have been here before,
  But when or how I cannot tell;
I know the grass beyond the door,
  The sweet keen smell.
The sighing sound, the lights around the shore.

You have been mine before,—
  How long ago I may not know:
But just when at that swallow's soar
  Your neck turned so,
Some veil did fall,—I knew it all of yore.

—Dante Gabriel Rossetti,
"Sudden Light"

*P*AST-LIFE regressions became extremely popular in the 1970s and the interest has remained high ever since. Twenty-five years ago it was relatively unusual for someone to come to me for a past-life regression. Nowadays, I can sometimes see three or four people in a single day.

There are a number of reasons for this. Interest in reincarnation is steadily growing and more people are becoming curious about what they did in their previous lifetimes. There is much more information about past lives in the popular press, and this has made people desire to seek out their own backgrounds. A number of film stars and other personalities have expressed a belief in reincarnation, and this has also created interest. As well, people who have been regressed to their previous lives talk about the experience, and this creates more interest, also.

People were conducting past-life regressions for almost a century before the sudden upsurge of interest in the seventies. A Spaniard called Colavida began experimenting with age regression in 1887. Dr. Mortis Stark is believed to have been the first to experiment with taking people back to their past lives. This was in 1906.[1] However, it is possible that he was not the first. The father of hypnotic regressions was Lieutenant-Colonel Albert de Rochas (1837–1914) who was a prolific author and psychic investigator. He first published his findings in 1911, but had been conducting research for many years prior to that. He performed countless past-life regressions, but was constantly frustrated by his inability to scientifically prove the veracity of the often detailed accounts of past lives that were told to him.

In his book, *Successive Lives,* Colonel de Rochas described his experiments with his cook, Josephine.[2] She was an excellent subject and provided detailed accounts of two previous incarnations. In one of these, she was a man named Jean Claude Bourdon, who was born in Champvent and had been in the Seventh Artillery regiment at Besançon. In her next life was a woman named Philomène Charpigny who married a man named Carteron. It was obvious that she knew nothing about either of these people and Colonel de Rochas spent several months checking out and confirming the details that she had provided. Although everything checked out perfectly, to de Rochas' chagrin, it was not considered proof of reincarnation.

One of Colonel de Rochas' best subjects was an eighteen-year-old girl named Marie Mayo. In one life she recalled the death of her husband in a shipwreck and how, in despair, she had thrown herself from the top of a cliff into the sea and drowned. She also remembered a life as Charles Mauville, a clerk in Paris during the reign of Louis XVII. He was a murderer and died at the age of fifty. In another lifetime she was Madeleine de Saint-Marc, the wife of a French nobleman. Colonel de Rochas went further than usual with Marie Mayo. One year later, he regressed her again, and found that she gave exactly the same details as before.[3]

Colonel de Rochas thought deeply about his past-life regressions and came up with four hypotheses to explain them. The first possibility was that the person was simply dreaming. However, de Rochas doubted that people could dream of several completely different previous lives. The second suggestion was that the person subconsciously gained information from his or her parents conversations. Again, de Rochas felt that this might explain one previous lifetime, but could not explain several. His third suggestion was that the person had learned a number of historical facts as he or she grew up, and used these to subconsciously create a past life. His final suggestion was that the person had actually lived in the past, and consequently, every bit of information that was provided needed be verified for accuracy.[4]

Colonel de Rochas played a major role in creating interest in past-life regressions. Unfortunately, he made one major mistake. He insisted that when he made longitudinal passes down the clients' bodies, they would go back to a past life, but when he made transverse passes they would progress into a future life. Other leading researchers of the day denied this, but Colonel de Rochas stubbornly insisted that it was so. This disagreement caused many people to dismiss the concept of reincarnation.

Since the time of de Rochas, many people in different parts of the world have investigated past-life regressions. In Sweden, John Björkhem (1910–1963) conducted hundreds of regressions and was able to verify many of the discoveries afterwards. Dr Alexander Cannon, a British psychiatrist, did his best to disprove the concept of reincarnation, but changed his mind after conducting more than a thousand hypnotic regressions. In Russia, Varvara Ivanova, conducted research on past-life regressions and came to the conclusion that we have to face the same problems again and again until we learn the lessons and master them.[5] More recently, the writings of Dr. Edith Fiore, Dr. Bruce Goldberg, Jeffrey Iverson, Dick Sutphen, Dr. Helen Wambach, and Dr. Brian L. Weiss have all played an important part in increasing public awareness of the veracity of past-life regressions.

Edgar Cayce, the "sleeping prophet," helped to increase interest in reincarnation. Over a period of twenty-one years, he gave some 2,500 "life readings" of people that included details of their past lives. This was initially an embarrassment to Cayce, who was a devout Christian, and read the entire Bible on a yearly basis for forty years. The Association for Research and Enlightenment (ARE) is dedicated to studying the findings that Edgar Cayce made. The fourteen million words he spoke while in trance were recorded on more than 90,000 typewritten pages. The index alone is stored on more than two hundred thousand cards. Some years ago, I was privileged to see them when I visited the ARE in Virginia Beach, Virginia.

Undoubtedly, the most famous case of a past-life regression is that of Bridey Murphy. In 1952, Morey Bernstein, a young Colorado businessman, was experimenting with hypnosis and thought it would be interesting to see if it was possible to take people back before birth and see what memories could be found. Interestingly enough, it was a book on the subject by Dr. Alexander Cannon that sparked his interest. The person who agreed to be regressed was Virginia Tighe, a young married woman. (In the best-selling book that Morey Bernstein wrote about his findings, she is known as Ruth Simmons. This was done to protect her privacy.[6]) She proved to be an excellent subject and in six tape-recorded sessions regressed back to a life as Bridey Murphy in nineteenth-century Ireland. She was born in County Cork in 1798, the daughter of Duncan and Kathleen Murphy, and her full name was Bridget Kathleen Murphy. Her father was a barrister, and she had an older brother named Duncan, and a younger brother who died as a baby. Until the age of fifteen she went to a school run by a Mrs. Strayne, and her brother later married Mrs. Strayne's daughter. Although she was a Protestant, Bridey married Sean Joseph MacCarthy, a Catholic, and they had two wedding ceremonies, one in Cork and the other in Belfast. Her husband was a lawyer, who later taught law at Queens University in Belfast. Bridey had no children and died at the age of sixty-six after falling down a flight of stairs.

Unfortunately, no records of births, marriages. or death were kept in Ireland until 1864, the year Bridey died, and these details were not able to be verified. However, the stores that Bridey mentioned all existed. The quaint Irish brogue that she spoke in contained numerous words that are no longer spoken, but were in common use at the time. For instance she used the word "brates" (a wishing cup), "lough" (a lake or river), and "flats" (platters). She accurately described the furniture, coinage, kitchen utensils, dances of the day, books, and even the new street lighting in Belfast. Although people have tried to disprove her story, it is hard to deny the incredible amount of accurate detail that came through during the regressions. To finish off one session she performed "The Morning Jig," and correctly gave a comic yawn at the end.

One detail the skeptics seized upon was Bridey's description of a metal bed as it was thought that they were not used in Ireland until 1850. However, research showed that they had been advertised as far back as 1802. Gradually, the skepticism faded as more and more details were verified. William J. Barker, a reporter on the *Denver Post* spent three weeks in Ireland and became convinced that the essential facts were true. He wrote a 19,000-word report on the case which was published as a twelve-page supplement in the newspaper on March 11, 1956. Later editions of Morey Bernstein's book contain an additional two chapters by William Barker which outlines the evidence he found and refutes the ignorant suppositions of the reporters who claimed it was all a hoax.[7]

Morey Bernstein's book, *The Search for Bridey Murphy*, sold more than a million copies and later became a successful movie. It also started a reincarnation craze, described by *Life* magazine as a "hypnotizzy." The book was serialized in more than fifty newspapers. A documentary movie was made, and a long-playing record of one of the trance sessions sold tens of thousands of copies. People wrote songs on the subject ("Do You Believe in Reincarnation," "The Love of Bridey Murphy," and "The Bridey Murphy Rock and Roll"), held "come as you were" parties, and even invented cocktails on the theme.

Twenty years later, the famous "Bloxham Tapes" created almost as much interest. Arnall Bloxham was a Cardiff hypnotherapist who had regressed people for more than twenty years. He was a reputable man who had always believed in reincarnation. He served as president of the British Society of Hypnotherapists in 1972.

Over the years, he had built up a valuable collection of more than four hundred tape recordings of the sessions. Jeffrey Iverson, a BBC television producer, heard about them quite casually at a party in 1974. He was always searching for interesting subjects and paid a visit on the elderly hypnotherapist who agreed to cooperate in a television documentary. After listening to the tapes, Jeffrey Iverson selected the ones that he thought could be verified. Two of Arnall Bloxham's best subjects, Jane Evans and Graham Huxtable, agreed to appear on the program and be regressed to their past lives. Graham Huxtable regressed to a life as a seaman on a Royal Navy frigate that fought against the French. Jane Evans regressed back to seven different lifetimes. In three of them, the detail was incredible. The earliest of these was set in York, three hundred years B.C.E. In that lifetime she was called Livonia and was married to Titus, who was tutor to the youngest son of Constantius, the governor of Britain.

Her next major lifetime was also spent in York, in 1190, she was called Rebecca and was married to Joseph, a rich Jewish moneylender. Anti-Jewish feelings were strong and the family was forced to flee after bandits broke into the house next door and killed the inhabitants. Unfortunately, they had waited too long and were only able to flee as far as the castle of York. Finally, they found refuge in the crypt beneath a church. Soldiers found the family and they were all killed.

Her last major life was spent as a young Egyptian servant, named Alison, in medieval France. She was a member of the household of Jacques Coeur, a wealthy merchant prince. She knew all about his intrigues and his fall from grace, after the king's mistress died. There were rumors that Jacques Coeur had poisoned her, and he was eventually arrested and imprisoned. Before this happened, he gave Alison some poison and she killed herself after he was arrested.

All of these exciting accounts created huge public interest when shown on Jeffrey Iverson's television documentary *More Lives Than One*. This was also the title of a well-known book he later wrote on the subject.[8] Again the skeptics came out in force, but although they were able to provide possible alternatives for many of the stories, there were vital incidents that had no explanation.

For instance, at the time the documentary was made, no one believed that there were crypts beneath any church in York, let alone the church that had been identified as the one where Rebecca and her family had sheltered. The actual crypt was discovered only after the television program had been shown.[9]

My first researches into soul mates were done as part of my hypnotherapy practice. Most of my clients wanted to control stress, lose weight, or stop smoking, but a steady stream of people were interested in having past-life regressions. A few of these people were simply curious about reincarnation and wanted to see where they had been and what they had done in previous incarnations. Most of the others wanted the regression to see if their current relationship was with the same person they had been with in previous lifetimes.

I found the regressions fascinating. My clients obviously did also, as many of them returned many times, either to examine different lifetimes or to more fully explore a particular incarnation.

One man has come to me regularly for more than fifteen years. Jim is a carpenter who became interested in his previous lives when a customer commented on how good he was with his hands. This customer told him that he must have developed those skills over many lifetimes. We have explored literally dozens of his previous lifetimes. Jim has always been a practical person with hands that could virtually think for themselves. We have explored just as many lifetimes when he was a woman as we have when he was a man. This disturbed him at first, as he is very much a "macho" man, but he is more intrigued with the fact that he has been so intensely practical and inventive in every lifetime.

Although Jim had strong relationships in most of his previous lives, none of them seem to have lasted more than one lifetime. I felt that there was a karmic factor present as in some of his male lifetimes he badly abused women, but also frequently suffered that same abuse in his lifetimes as a woman. Usually, a karmic debt of this sort is played out between the same two people over many lifetimes. However, not one of Jim's many relationships could be classified as a soul mate one. In this current lifetime he has been divorced and has no plans to marry again, as he still carries much bitterness about the way his marriage ended. He is coming to terms with the fact that he is learning karmic lessons, and I have noticed his attitude toward women has changed enormously over the time I have known him.

I found it intriguing that this man, who has had countless relationships over the last few thousand years, has never found his soul mate. We conducted several regressions to see if we had somehow overlooked or not found any pertinent lifetimes. We found a number of people who appeared in many lifetimes, but they never figured in a romantic role. His mother in this lifetime, for instance, has been his mother several times before, but she has also been his brother, sister, and cousin, as well as his employer. However, we uncovered nothing that related to a romantic soul mate relationship of any sort.

Fortunately, this man seems to be an exception. Most people I have regressed have had no difficulty in recognizing special people from this current lifetime in previous incarnations, even though the sexes and relationships may be totally different.

One example is a women in her middle thirties who came to me originally to stop smoking. By chance, a program on past lives was shown on television a day or two after she had been to me. She called me the next morning to see if I could take her back to a past life.

She regressed quickly and easily to a previous incarnation in rural France in the late nineteenth century. Life was difficult and the family had to work extremely hard to survive. However, they were a close family and were extremely happy. In this past life she was the oldest child in a large family. One of her brothers in that lifetime is her sister in this one. Her father was a boy who lived next door, and was considered virtually part of the family. Her mother fulfilled the same role in both lifetimes. However, her husband in this lifetime was the person she had loved in the previous incarnation, but the love was never consummated as he was married to her best friend (who is her son in this lifetime).

This lady was excited with her regression. Although she had come to me out of curiosity, she was thrilled that she and her husband were soul mates, even though the relationship had been impossible during that lifetime. She was also highly intrigued that her husband in this lifetime had been married to their son, as it helped to explain the close bond between father and son, as well as her constant difficulties with him.

She came back for further regressions, and we found several lifetimes where she and her husband had been together. They had been brother and sister at one time, and husband and wife in three others. In one of those, she had been the husband and he had been the wife.

We also uncovered a lifetime in which her husband did not figure. In that lifetime, in twelfth-century Rome, she was the daughter of a wealthy merchant. She lived a life of luxury, and had many suitors, but did not marry. Her overwhelming impression of that lifetime was a sickening feeling of loneliness that felt like a pain in her stomach. She had constant pressure put on her by her family who wanted her to marry certain suitors for business and political reasons, but she had been strong enough to resist.

By this time, the lady had become so enthralled with her regressions that she forced her husband to come for a regression. I was not overly happy about this, as people can only enter trance easily, if they want to do it. However, I need not have worried. He was an excellent subject and his regression confirmed much of what his wife had already learned.

Just for interest, I took him back to the twelfth century to see why it was that he had not figured in his wife's incarnation at that time.

He had been the son of a wealthy merchant in Venice. In the normal scheme of things, the two of them might easily have met, as a merger of the two wealthy families would have created a powerful and influential business. However, at the age of sixteen, he had been seduced by his uncle. The knowledge that he was homosexual had been so devastating that he had committed suicide.

It appears that everything had been in place for the two to meet, but fate had stepped in at the last minute. Thinking that there must be a karmic explanation for what had happened, I regressed him back one further lifetime. In that life, a century earlier in Greece, he had loathed and detested homosexuals. When he discovered that a childhood friend of his was gay, he had ridiculed and persecuted his former friend so much that he was forced to leave home, never to return. It is likely that the bad karma he received from this was repaid in the following lifetime, which meant that he died before meeting his soul mate.

In *Spirit Guides and Angel Guardians*, I related an incident where a woman regressed back to a past life and found that her mother in that lifetime was her spirit guide in this incarnation.[10] A spirit guide is someone who has died but retains an interest in the well-being of someone who is currently alive. A spirit guide is usually, but not always, a deceased relative, which explains why many of my clients over the years have been able to recognize a spirit guide while exploring their past lives. A spirit guide is mainly concerned with the person's spiritual growth, but can be called upon for help at any time.

I had another interesting instance of this several months ago. A man came to me for a past-life regression. His sister had been to me a week earlier, so I assumed that he was coming out of curiosity. However, when he arrived, he told me that all his life he had had a spirit guide who had helped him immensely. He had never been able to see his guide, though, and hoped that this person might appear in a regression.

He proved to be a good subject and returned easily to a life as a fisherman in a Polynesian island. Life was good, and he had a strong relationship and many children. Occasionally, he would get drunk and beat up his children, but apart from that, he appeared to lead a model life. He died in his middle fifties of drowning, when a sudden storm came up before he could return to land. I asked him direct questions about his spirit guide, but in the regression he did not appear to understand what I was asking him.

However, when he came out of trance and returned to the present he was excited. In the life we explored, he had been extremely proud of his oldest son, and this person was his spirit guide in this lifetime.

"How do you know?" I asked.

The man smiled. "It's strange, but as soon as I saw him, I knew who it was. He was my child, of course, even though he is my guide and mentor this time, but there was a sudden sense of knowing. I'm thrilled to know what he looks like."

Hypnotic regressions are always fascinating but can sometimes produce inconclusive results. Some years ago, I was conducting a session with a man needing help with confidence and self-esteem. During the session, he spontaneously regressed into a past life. This happens occasionally, and sometimes people become so startled that they come out of hypnosis. However, my client seemed perfectly happy and I thought I would use the opportunity to see if his lack of confidence related to something that had occurred during this previous lifetime.

He had been a wheelwright in a small village somewhere in Europe, probably in the sixteenth or seventeenth centuries. He was illiterate and could not tell me either the year or country he was in. He had been overpowered and intimidated by his father throughout his childhood and had grown up to be a timid, quiet man. People constantly took advantage of him, and he was owed money by many people who laughed at his attempts to get paid. He was in love with a young woman he had never spoken to. He was too shy and scared to initiate conversation. He lived a long, sad, and lonely life.

I thought that he would have been interested in the fact that his lack of confidence stemmed from the brutal treatment he had received as a child in this previous life-time. However, he was much more interested in the fact that the girl he had loved from afar was his wife in this lifetime.

A week or two later, his wife came in for a regression. We uncovered a number of previous lifetimes in Europe at the approximate time that her husband had indicated, but could not find a lifetime where the two of them were together.

I puzzled about this for a long time, as it appeared from the husband's involuntary regression that the couple were soul mates, but he did not figure in any of his wife's previous lifetimes. Unfortunately for me, the man did not want to explore the matter further, and I did no further regressions with him.

Sometimes it is difficult to determine who the person's soul mate is, as frequently entire families figure in each regression. As the relationships and sexes change, the person being regressed could have a deep, loving, intimate relationship with the every member of the family over a period of many incarnations.

However, I believe that we are not limited to one soul mate, and this is probably evidence of this.

A lady I know called Lynda has been married twice and is convinced that both of her husbands are her soul mates. Her first husband died tragically when his small boat capsized when he was out fishing. He was only thirty-six, and his wife was pregnant with their third child. Three years later, Lynda met her second husband while picking up her son from school. She had noticed the tall, studious-looking man waiting for his daughter on several occasions, but this day they happened to be standing side by side. He initiated a conversation, and the immediate bond between them was so instant that it startled them both.

"It was as if I was meeting an old friend again," Lynda told me. "The bond and rapport were there from the second we met, and we seemed to be able to discuss everything together."

They married three months later, despite the objections of well-meaning friends who thought they were rushing in to it too quickly. They have experienced the usual ups and downs of married life, but the unusually close bond they have, coupled with their ability to discuss everything freely, has ensured the success of the relationship.

On their tenth wedding anniversary, Lynda's husband paid for her to have a regression. In her past life, Lynda was a preacher's daughter in the deep South. She had a happy childhood growing up in a small town where everyone knew everyone else. Living next door were two boys, one the same age as her and the other two years older. As children they were inseparable. Lynda was convinced that when she grew up she'd marry one or the other. In fact, she married neither, as the boys moved to another town when she was sixteen. They lost contact with each other for forty years. Lynda met one of them again when visiting her grandchildren. She stopped at a store to buy a present, and the owner turned out to be the older of the two brothers. He was divorced, but Lynda was still married. All the same, a close friendship began again and lasted until he died a few years later.

Lynda was excited with her regression as the two brothers were her two husbands in this incarnation.

"It's so strange," she said. "In that lifetime I wanted to marry both of them, and ended up with neither. In this lifetime I've married them both!"

Past-life regressions are an effective way of seeing if important people in this current life played important roles in previous lifetimes.

They can also be helpful in other ways. For instance, you may have an unexplained memory that can be resolved easily during a past-life regression. All of my life I've had a memory of being a small child sitting in front of a huge fire, while circles of red danced around and around. This memory made no sense to me, as it was not something that related to my present life. However, one day, I reached for an encyclopedia while helping my older son with his homework. The book opened on a page showing Russian peasant women dancing around a fire. Their dresses were black on the outside, but the inner lining was red. As a small child, lying half asleep beside the fire, all I could see was the circles of red made by the inner lining as the women danced. I immediately regressed myself back to the past life where this experience occurred, and am now familiar with much of what happened to me during that lifetime.

If you have any unexplained memories, you do not need to wait until you chance upon an explanation, as I did. Simply regress yourself back to the time when that memory occurred, and the meaning of it all will become clear.

Although it is easier to visit a competent hypnotherapist for a past-life regression, it is not hard to regress yourself and explore your own past lives. We will be doing this in chapter 7.

Getting Ready

What your heart thinks great, is great. The soul's emphasis is always right.

—Ralph Waldo Emerson[1]

$\mathcal{T}$HERE ARE a number of things that have to be done before you can start attracting your soul mate to you. The most important factor is to know yourself well enough to understand what your real needs are. Many people try to hide from these, and instead choose someone in an attempt to please someone else. You will not find a lasting relationship by trying to please your parents, other relatives, or friends. Any relationship that is based on pleasing others is doomed to failure. You not only need to find someone who will make you happy, for total fulfillment you need to find your soul mate. Total honesty with yourself is essential when searching for your soul mate. Some people write down a list of their requirements in a partner. If you think this will be helpful, it is worth doing, but only as long as you are totally honest with yourself.

Not long ago, a man came to me for hypnotherapy. He had been married twice before, each time to extremely slim women. However, even when making love to his former wives, he fantasized about sleeping with larger women. He had now met such a person, and was deeply in love with her. However, he felt embarrassed about the idea of being seen in public with her. He worried about what his friends and colleagues would think or say. In other words, he was letting the opinions of other people decide who would be a suitable partner for him. Until he came to realize this, and decide whether or not the opinions of others mattered, he was miserable. Fortunately, after a couple of sessions, he realized that his personal happiness was much more important than the comments of others, and he proposed to his new love. Now that he is finally being honest with himself, I am sure he will be extremely happy.

This man reminded me of Hermia's comment in Shakespeare's *A Midsummer Night's Dream* when she said: "O hell, to choose love by another's eyes!" People were doing it years before Shakespeare was born, and sadly, they are still doing it today. Fortunately, my client learned this lesson in time.

You need to be ready—physically, mentally, emotionally, and spiritually. Any one of these areas can create a blockage of energies that will prevent you from contacting your soul mate.

It is important that you feel ready for a soul mate relationship. If you are not yet ready to settle down, or enjoy playing the field too much, do not try to attract a soul mate. Wait until you feel ready to have someone special in your life.

Jason, an acquaintance of mine, is in his early thirties. He was married to a beautiful woman for three years, but the relationship ended when she discovered he was having affairs with other women. Since his divorce he has been sleeping with as many women as he can. Jason is a good-looking, charming man, and never lacks female company. He would be the first to agree that he is simply satisfying his lust. He has no feelings for any of the women, and admits that he is simply, as he puts it, "putting notches on my belt."

Recently, he confided in me that he was getting less and less satisfaction from his conquests, and that maybe the time had come for him to seek out his soul mate. This was simply an idle thought on his part, though, as I have seen him with several other women since then. At the moment, Jason is not ready to attract a soul mate to himself. He will need to mature, and be prepared to put his bachelor lifestyle behind him, before he starts a serious search for his soul mate.

Veronica, who works in an office supply company near my home, is in her late forties. She has two grown-up children, and has recently separated from her husband. He abused her, physically and verbally, throughout their twenty-five year marriage. Consequently, she has totally lost confidence in herself, and is living a lonely life on her own. She would love to find her soul mate, but is also not ready yet. For one thing, she repels any approaches by men. This is not surprising, because of what she has been through, but it means that she might accidentally turn away the perfect man. Veronica will have to build up her self-esteem and confidence, develop some social skills, and become more positive about her life before starting to attract a soul mate.

The Physical You

Even if you are not physically fit now, no doubt there was a time when you were physically fit and active. When you are physically fit, you are able to accomplish things more easily. You are likely to feel good about yourself, and have more than enough energy to do anything you set your mind on.

You cannot expect to attract the perfect soul mate to you if you are a couch potato and spend several hours a day lying on the sofa watching television. There is definitely a time to rest and relax, and television can be wonderful for that, but if you are spending untold hours staring blankly at whatever happens to be on at the time, you will not be in good shape to attract a soul mate.

The problem with spending too much time lazing around doing nothing is that you become lethargic and lacking in life and energy. You cannot attract anything worthwhile to you while you are in this state.

Resolve to become more active. Go for walks, join a gym, do something. Who knows, your soul mate might already be at the gym waiting for you. If you continue staring blankly at the small screen you will never meet him or her.

Use, don't waste, your energy. Have you ever noticed how much energy small children have? They appear to have limitless reserves. Of course, they don't, but they sleep and rest and then start over again. Every time you waste energy, you are using up calories.

Many years ago, someone told me that we all have a danger level. Once we get past it, it becomes extremely difficult to regain our lost vigor. The danger level occurs when you are sitting down comfortably and want to read the newspaper, which is only a few yards away. Instead of getting up to get it, you say, "Honey, would you pass me the paper?" Consequently, someone else gets to use up a few calories, while you become more entrenched in your sedentary lifestyle.

I am not expecting you go out and start running marathons. If you are currently leading an inactive lifestyle, I am suggesting that you move around a bit more, and learn to experience the joys of exercise. Start slowly. It makes no difference how little you do to start with, as long as you gradually extend it. A woman once told me that she had started off with two-minute walks. She would walk for one minute and then turn around and come back. Then she extended it to two minutes each way, and now she walks for an hour every day, and is enjoying the benefits it brings to her life.

At one lecture I gave, an obese man asked me if it was worth bothering with exercise as it was possible that his soul mate might also be overweight. Of course, anything is possible. However, he still needed to lose some weight, as by doing so he would gain more energy and would be motivated to attract a soul mate to him.

Most people simply need to lose a few pounds to get into reasonable shape. Once you have done this, you will feel much better about yourself, and will be physically ready to attract your soul mate to you. You certainly do not have to look like a fashion model. As long as you feel active, and do not feel embarrassed about the way you look, you are ready to start.

The Mental You

Your mental outlook is also important. We attract to us what we think about. If you think that you will never find your soul mate, you are correct. If you know that you will attract your soul mate to you, you are just as correct.

Positive thinking is essential. This can be hard if you have been searching for your soul mate for a long time. However, remaining positively expectant is by far the best way to attract the right person to you.

We are all our own worst enemies at times. It is important that whenever you find yourself thinking negative thoughts that you simply turn them around and make them positive. Do not berate yourself or become annoyed. Just consciously stop your negative thinking, and replace any negative thoughts with positive ones. Over a period of time you will amaze yourself with the positive changes in your life simply by doing this. When you think positively, you become a magnet that draws positive and beneficial things into your life.

The Emotional You

Our emotions are frequently hard to handle. A friend of mine has tried to control his overwhelming feelings of jealousy for more than twenty years. These unbidden, emotionally crippling feelings catch him time and time again, and he seems powerless to prevent them. Over the years, it has cost him several relationships and at least one job.

However, although it has taken him more than twenty years, he is much more in control of his feelings now than ever before. In the past he would feel jealous if his partner even looked at another man. Today he is quite at ease if they go to a party and she spends most of the night talking to other people.

He still suffers jealousy in other ways, though. When a colleague was promoted ahead of him, he felt profoundly jealous. Even while experiencing these feelings, he realized that it was his overpowering emotions that had cost him the position. When his next-door neighbor bought a new car, he felt jealous.

"Something like that shouldn't affect me at all," he told me. "It's irrational and stupid. But I get churned up over it, all the same." Obviously, learning to harness and control his emotions is an important part of what my friend has to learn in this lifetime.

We are all emotional creatures. Few people suffer from their emotions to the extent of my friend, but all of our emotions send out powerful energies that affect and influence everyone in our lives. Our emotions color everything we do. Good, positive emotions make every day a joyful one, but negative emotions can transform a heaven into a living hell.

Become aware of your emotions and the effect they have on others. Encourage the good emotions, and pay special attention to the negative ones. It is probably unrealistic to totally eliminate them, but concentrate on controlling them. By doing this every aspect of your life will improve.

The Spiritual You

Most of us live in the physical world and pay little attention to the spiritual side of our lives. It has become a cliché to say that we are spiritual beings enjoying a physical incarnation. Yet we attract our soul mate to us on the spiritual and soul levels. The desire for a soul mate begins at these levels. Consequently, we need to pay close attention to our soul. Our soul knows what we need, and will bring it to us if we desire it enough.

At the same time, your soul mate, who you may not have met yet, will also be sending out his or her desires on the soul level. In many ways, it is like two magnets that attract each other.

Your Soul

Finally, you need to be at peace with your own soul. If you are not in contact with your own soul, how can anyone else reach it? It is not easy to become in tune with your own soul. It is largely a matter of feeling at peace and in tune with the infinite. In many ways, awareness of the soul is a culmination and combination of our physical, mental, emotional, and spiritual selves. It is a matter of being and doing the best we can at all times.

We also need to be fair, honest, and ethical, and lead a life of peace and calm. Jesus said: "For what is a man profited, if he shall gain the whole world, and lose his own soul? or what shall a man give in exchange for his soul?" (Matthew 16:26).

Jesus also said: "But seek ye first the kingdom of God, and his righteousness; and all these things shall be added unto you" (Matthew 6:33). By finding God, whoever or whatever that means to you, you will also find peace for your soul.

The Types of Love

Love is the most powerful force in the universe. It is also an essential ingredient in leading a happy, fulfilling life. Numerous illnesses can be put down to a lack of love, both given and received. In fact, lack of love has caused the death of countless people throughout history. This should never happen, as we can easily generate love inside ourselves to send out to the universe. It is tragic that so many people around the world are desperately craving love.

There are two types of love, personal and impersonal. Personal love is love between two people, and is the type of love we are focusing on in this book. Impersonal love is the empathy and concern that we should express to everyone we come in contact with. It could be described as the ability to get along with others.

There is a law of reciprocity in the universe. We get back what we put out. If we want love in our loves, both personal and impersonal, we need to generate love inside ourselves so that we can give it freely to others. By doing this, we also attract love to us. We cannot expect love first. We need to give it out, in order to receive it back. There is a saying that goes: "Love wasn't put in your heart to stay. Love isn't love until you give it away." Ralph Waldo Emerson expressed the same thought when he wrote: "Love, and you shall be loved. All love is mathematically just, as much as the two sides of an algebraic equation."[2]

There is an interesting experiment that I frequently ask my students to try. I suggest that for one week they smile at everyone they come across. This includes strangers they see on the street. A week later I ask them what happened. Without exception, they tell me that most people smiled back. If they had not smiled first, they would have received few smiles during the week. Smiling costs nothing, but makes everyone feel better. I even recall reading a newspaper story about a man who was suicidal, but was saved by the smile of a stranger on the street.

The purpose of this exercise is not to demonstrate the power of a smile, although it certainly does show that. I ask my students to do it to teach them that they have to give first before they can receive.

It is a simple matter to generate love inside ourselves. No matter what disappointments or setbacks you have had in the past, you can still create love. You might be thoroughly disillusioned and feel skeptical about the whole idea of love, but you can still create it.

Love comes from within and is expressed in our thoughts, feelings, conversations, and actions. As you start doing this consciously, you will notice subtle changes in your life and attitude. Things that were formerly difficult suddenly become easy, and you will find yourself becoming more confident and sure of yourself.

In a short space of time you will find yourself expressing love in everything you do.

I find affirmations extremely helpful in generating love. Affirmations are simply words that you repeat to yourself on a regular basis. I say affirmations to myself whenever I am waiting in line or held up in traffic. Situations such as these used to annoy me, but now I am content to wait as long as is necessary as I can make productive use of the time.

You can create affirmations to cover any aspect of your life you wish to improve. They should be composed in the present tense and state exactly what it is that you desire. For instance, if you are desperately poor, you might say to yourself: "I have all the money that I need." At the time you say this, this is obviously not true. However, your subconscious mind does not know that. It simply accepts the thoughts that are put into it and acts on that information. In time, your subconscious mind will make that affirmation become a reality.

Consequently, if you want more love in your life, you might say: "I am a good and loving person. I love life. I attract good, loving people into my life. My life is rich in love and happiness. I experience love in everything that I say and do."

Impersonal love also responds well to affirmations. You might say: "I love everyone, and everyone loves me." Say this to yourself on a regular basis and you will find every aspect of your life gradually becoming smoother and easier.

Loving Yourself

I believe that low self-esteem and fear are the major reasons so many people find it hard to attract the right relationship to them. We attract to us what we think about. If we think that we are worthless and unlovable, it is impossible to attract the right person to us. If we are fearful and insecure, we tend to insulate ourselves away from the world and miss out on the many opportunities that are always there for meeting other people. We can only overcome low self-esteem and fear by loving ourselves.

There is truth as well as cynicism in Oscar Wilde's often-quoted remark: "To love oneself is the beginning of a lifelong romance." Although this might at first glance seem like selfishness, it is vital that you love yourself. You are the only person that you can guarantee you will be spending the rest of your life with. Consequently, you should not only *like* yourself, but you should *love* yourself as well. By loving yourself you will gain trust, self-acceptance, and self-worth.

You love yourself by being kind to yourself, by nurturing yourself, by liking yourself, by forgiving yourself. You need to accept yourself as you are now, and allow yourself to become your own best friend.

By doing this, you will generate love, not only for yourself, but for others as well.

A useful exercise to help you love yourself is to spend a minute or two each day looking at yourself in the mirror.

Become in tune with yourself, and allow whatever thoughts, feelings, or emotions occur to come to the surface. Some will be happy, but others will be sad. Have fun doing this exercise. Make faces at yourself, smile, laugh, and perform funny gestures and movements.

Many people find it hard to do this exercise. We all look at our reflections in the mirror when we are brushing our hair, putting on makeup, shaving, or checking our appearance. However, many people feel that studying themselves in a mirror is simply being narcissistic. The purpose of this exercise is not to simply admire ourselves. We are looking beyond that, and allowing the real person—the vulnerable, real person that usually hides behind the mask of the face—to become visible.

To begin with, you will notice the lines, frown marks, and wrinkles on your face. Things that have always bothered you might be extremely obvious. You might think your nose is too large, or your mouth too small. However, in time, you will look beyond these things, and achieve self-acceptance, an inner peace, and a love for yourself and others. This exercise is, in reality, a form of meditation.

Incidentally, I have spoken to a surprising number of people who first saw their soul mates while doing this exercise. When they looked in the mirror, they saw, not their reflection, but the image of the soul mate they had yet to meet. This is not likely to happen the first, or even twentieth, time you do this exercise. However, it is something to have at the back of your mind. The people who experienced this all told me how helpful it had been. They all, without exception, met their soul mate within six months of first seeing him or her in their mirror.

You would not be reading this book if you did not want to attract the perfect person into your life. Pay attention to your physical, mental, emotional, and spiritual bodies. Become in tune with your soul and send out love. By doing this you will become a powerful magnet that will attract to you everything that you desire.

It is not easy to make yourself ready on every level. It takes time and effort. It may seem like too much work, particularly if you feel that more than one level needs attention. We need to become the very best person that we can be, on every level. Try and look at yourself as others see you. Are people attracted to you, or do they tend to avoid you? Naturally, you want to be the very best you that is possible, to help attract your soul mate. In the process, you will also attract many other people into your life, and your life will become fuller and more rewarding in many different ways.

Baggage Release Exercise

We all carry around with us a mountain of baggage from the past. These might be resentments, unresolved issues, ancient wrongs, things we should have done or said, and so on. We might be so weighed down with these that we cannot progress any further with our lives.

Fortunately, there is a simple exercise you can do to let go of all of this rubbish from the past. This exercise allows you to eliminate all of the negative energies that are slowing you down and concealing your inner beauty.

Find a quiet, warm place where you will not be disturbed. If you are doing this indoors, you might want to temporarily disconnect the telephone.

Sit back in a comfortable chair, or lie down, if preferred. Close your eyes and take ten deep breaths. As you exhale, say to yourself, "Relax, relax, relax." Allow all of the muscles of your body to relax. Once you have taken the ten breaths, forget about your breathing and become aware of any areas of tension in your body. Consciously relax these areas. Pay particular attention to your shoulders, as tension and stress often gather there.

Once you are totally relaxed, visualize yourself in the most peaceful place you can imagine. You might picture yourself lying on a beautiful beach, listening to the waves. You might prefer to place yourself in a little grove in the middle of a forest. It makes no difference where you go, just as long as it makes you feel totally relaxed.

Visualize yourself in this restful, relaxing place. Then, imagine that your body is turning into a large ball. Picture yourself looking like a huge ball of twine. Extending from this ball are countless threads leading outwards to all of the unwanted baggage that we are still holding on to.

See this picture as clearly as you can in your mind. Take an imaginary pair of scissors and cut off all of the threads, until your ball is smooth and round again. Enjoy the sight of this perfect ball, and then watch it turn back into you again. However, the person you return to is different from the person you were before. You are now free of all the unnecessary baggage you have been carrying around for years, or even decades.

Enjoy being in your restful scene for another minute or two, and then, when you feel ready, open your eyes. You will feel an incredible sense of release and freedom afterwards. Remember to do this exercise every now and then, as we all pick up unwanted baggage as we go through life. Doing this exercise regularly allows us to let go of the baggage sooner, rather than later.

Remember, though, that you cannot cut your family loose in this exercise. No matter what problems you may have with a parent or other relative, you must learn to handle it, as that is a karmic responsibility. Forgiveness can be just as healing as the baggage release exercise, and makes a good remedy for difficulties with family members. Letting go of unwanted baggage will improve every aspect of your life, as well as making it much easier to attract your soul mate to you. There is a simple exercise to verify that you are ready to welcome your soul mate into your life. Go somewhere on your own where you will not be disturbed or distracted. It makes no difference if you are indoors or outside.

Attraction Exercise

Close your eyes and relax as much as you possibly can. In your mind's eye, visualize your physical self. See your body as clearly as you can. As soon as the picture is clear in your mind, ask your heart if your physical body is ready for a soul mate. Your heart will respond. The response can come in a number of ways. If the answer is positive, you might feel a warmth or a glowing sensation in the area of your heart. You might experience a feeling of knowing that the answer is positive. Your whole body might give an involuntary sigh, as it accepts that you are physically ready for a soul mate. If the answer is negative, you may feel that your heart is repelling the thought. You might feel nothing at all, which means that your heart is not responding in a positive manner, indicating a negative reply. Naturally, if the answer is negative, you will have to do whatever is necessary to your physical body before asking again.

If you received a positive answer to the first question, you can then proceed to the next question. Visualize your mental self as clearly as you can. It is hard to describe your mental self, as the way you visualize it is likely to be completely different to the way I visualize my mental self. I see it as a pool of knowledge. I am continually adding to it as I learn and grow. When I am not learning, this pool is likely to become stagnant, so I try to add to it all the time. Many people see their mental bodies as their brains, and visualize this in their minds. Nowadays, many people tell me that they see their mental bodies as an incredibly powerful computer. Over the years, the range of answers I have had when asking people how they visualized their mental bodies has been astonishing.

Once you can clearly see your mental body, ask your heart if your mental body is ready to welcome a soul mate into your life. Remain calm, and wait for your heart to respond. If you receive a positive answer, you can proceed to the next question. If the answer is negative, you might want to relax for a while longer and ask yourself what you can do for your mental self to encourage a positive response.

If the range of visualizations of mental bodies was large, the range of emotional bodies is incredible. It seems that no two people visualize their emotional bodies in exactly the same way. Do not try to logically work out what your emotional body will look like. Wait until you do this exercise and see what comes into your mind. I was surprised to find that my emotional body is similar to an aura that entirely surrounds my physical body. It shimmers and is in a state of constant motion. Your emotional body is likely to be completely different.

Again, once you can visualize your emotional body, ask your heart if you are emotionally ready for your soul mate. If the answer is negative, your heart will respond in some way. It will not simply ignore the question, as it may have done with the physical and mental bodies.

After receiving a positive response to the emotional body, you can visualize your spiritual body. Your background and upbringing are likely to play a part in how you visualize your spiritual body. Ask if you are spiritually ready for a soul mate, and wait quietly until you receive an answer.

I am frequently asked what we can do if the spiritual body gives a negative answer. Naturally, the answer is to develop spiritually. This can be done in many ways. You should become more open to the needs of others, and be willing to help whenever necessary. You can read, study, meditate, and pray. In your prayers, ask for guidance and help in attracting a soul mate to you. Strive to become a beautiful person inwardly. Although this is inside you, the results will be clearly visible to everyone. You will develop calmness, serenity, and a quiet confidence that the universe is unfolding in exactly the way it should be. Once you feel you have made progress in this area go through the entire exercise again, starting with your physical body.

Finally, you need to visualize your soul. Of course, your soul is divine and without form, so you will not be able to see your actual soul. However, for the purposes of this exercise it is important to visualize it in any shape or form that you wish. I picture my soul as a glowing orb of golden light. You may visualize it in a totally different way. That is not important. The important part is that you get a clear picture of it in your mind. Your soul is the magnet that attracts your soul mate to you. By this stage you have received a positive response from your physical, mental, emotional, and spiritual bodies. All you need do now is to ask your soul to attract the right person to you. Focus on this request for as long as you can. Finally, let it go, and enjoy the pleasant relaxation for a minute or two before opening your eyes. Tell no one what you have done. Simply get on with your life, confident that you have put into play the necessary energies to attract your soul mate to you.

It is unlikely that you will receive a positive answer to each level the first time you do this experiment. If you receive a negative answer at any level, do not repeat the experiment until after you have given the negative response some serious thought. Usually, there are things that you will need to do before attempting the experiment again. I have known people who have done this experiment three or four times in a single day. Naturally, they received the same negative response every time.

Everyone visualizes things differently. Some people are extremely visual and can see their different bodies and soul with incredible clarity. Others see them much more faintly, while others do not really see them at all. However, although they cannot see them, they develop a strong sense that they are there. They might even be able to mentally feel the different bodies, or experience them in other ways. No one way is any better than any other. We are all unique and respond to different things in different ways. This is one reason why it is best not to discuss this experiment with anyone else.

When I first began teaching these methods, we would discuss this experiment afterwards. The people who could see everything clearly often considered themselves to be much more advanced than the people who failed to see anything, but experienced it in other ways. In fact, no one was more advanced than anyone else, but the people who failed to "see" felt themselves to be failures. This is not the case. The way in which you experience this experiment is the right way for you. Naturally, as soon as I discovered this, we stopped discussing this experiment as a group.

While you are making the necessary changes, think about your soul mate. See if you can picture him or her in your mind. If you are naturally attracted to people with blonde hair, your soul mate is bound to be blonde also. Are you attracted to people who are tall and slim? If so, this is likely to be how your soul mate will be. Are you attracted to a certain type of music? Your soul mate will enjoy listening to the same music that you do. Do you enjoy movies, opera, or baseball? It is highly likely that your soul mate will, too. No matter what your interests are, they are probably shared by your soul mate. Build up a clear picture of your potential soul mate in your mind. Every night, picture your soul mate in your mind while drifting off to sleep. By doing this, you will be sending out a message to the universe, asking your soul mate to contact you.

You are also likely to experience vivid dreams about the two of you together. This is an extremely positive indication that your soul mate is not far away. The more vivid your dreams become, the closer your soul mate is.

Work on your physical, mental, emotional, and spiritual sides of your makeup, remain positively expectant, and get ready to welcome your soul mate into your life.

Your Soul Mate Needs

We all have different ideas about the perfect partner. Someone might desire someone who is a good conversationalist and an excellent dancer. Someone else might be looking for an extrovert with an offbeat sense of humor. A third person might be looking for someone who is glamorous, sexy, and enjoys cooking. You might be searching for someone with totally different qualities to these. Your individual preferences are important. If you desire an extroverted partner who enjoys social activities and end up with a quiet introvert who loves nothing more than quiet nights at home, you are bound to have problems.

As we mature our needs and desires change. Someone who is twenty years old will have a completely different idea of what he or she wants in a soul mate relationship than a forty-five-year old person will. Someone who is in his or her seventies will have different requirements again. It is important to clarify in your own mind exactly what you desire in your perfect soul mate.

Are you looking for companionship and quiet walks along the beach, or are you looking for an active sex partner? Maybe you want both. It does not matter what you want as long as it is clear in your mind what you are seeking. Once you have worked out exactly what qualities you desire in a soul mate you can send out a message to the universe requesting such a person to come into your life.

Duncan is someone I've known virtually all my life. We have never been close friends, but our paths have crossed on many occasions. I vividly remember how determined he was to make his first million by the age of twenty-five. He succeeded in this and ended up controlling a number of successful corporations. However, this brought him little satisfaction as in the process he had ignored every other aspect of life.

On a long plane flight Duncan watched a young couple who were deeply in love. He became aware of a deep emptiness inside himself that he had been trying to ignore for years. He had plenty of money, but in the whole world there was no one he could call a true friend. By the end of the flight he had done some deep soul-searching and made several important decisions. He was going to become physically fit again, he would take up some interests that were totally unrelated to work and money, and he would try to find a special woman to share his life.

He gave a great deal of thought to what he wanted in a partner. Although he did not know the term "soul mate," that is what he was looking for.

"I wanted someone special to share my life with," he told me years later. "She had to be physically attractive, but that was of lesser importance than her intelligence. I wanted someone I could enjoy long conversations with, someone who could talk freely about everything. We had to have similar interests, so that we could do them together. I wanted someone who could help me come out of my shell, so to speak. I've never been good in group situations. I wanted a partner who could mix comfortably with others, and who could help me become more relaxed in that sort of situation. And, of course, she also had to be sexually attractive."

Duncan found it difficult as he had focussed so much on his quest for power and money that he had missed out on much that most people take for granted. Duncan was awkward with women and found it hard to initiate a conversation that did not involve business. It took much searching and experimentation to find a hobby that interested him. He tried playing golf and tennis, but found them time-consuming and unenjoyable. He considered most things a waste of time because they took him away from potentially lucrative opportunities. Finally, he joined a model railway enthusiasts group and began spending most Sundays taking underprivileged children for rides on miniature steam trains. He particularly enjoyed interacting with young children. He also found that he lost his habitual reserve while sharing smiles and jokes with his young passengers.

One weekend, he noticed an attractively dressed woman watching him as he ushered small children into the little carriages for another ride. She stayed for about an hour. He desperately wanted to speak to her, but was too shy. When he finally built up enough courage, she had gone. However, she returned two weeks later, and this time, he was determined not to let the opportunity pass by. He asked one of the other volunteers to drive the train and went over to her.

"I saw you here the other week," he said. "Do you like trains?"

The woman laughed. "Not really," she said. "I just enjoy seeing the happiness on the faces of the children."

"That's what brought me here, too," he admitted. Before he knew it, he had arranged to take her out to dinner the following evening, and four months later they became engaged.

"I finally feel alive," he told me at their engagement party. "I used to be driven by some force inside me. I needed that plane flight to get my life into perspective."

They have now been married for more than ten years and are extremely happy. Duncan is able to run his businesses from home, and rarely works for more than forty hours a week. He still enjoys the miniature trains, and most weekends his wife is there with him.

It is interesting to note that sexual attraction was of less importance to Duncan than intelligence and similar interests. If he had been twenty years younger it is likely that his list of attributes would have been completely different. Although Duncan had not been consciously looking for a soul mate, he had built up a list of attributes that he particularly desired, and by dwelling on them, had sent the message out. Several months later, his soul mate arrived. If he had remained focused only on money and business, it is unlikely that he would ever have met his soul mate.

4

Is There More Than One Soul Mate for Me?

Life is a flower of which love is the honey.
—Victor Hugo

MANY PEOPLE feel that there is only one potential soul mate for them in the whole world. Fortunately, this is not the case. It would be terrible if you lived in Iowa, but your one and only soul mate lived in Finland. It is highly likely that you will find a soul mate in the town or city you already live in. You do not need to relocate halfway around the world to be with your soul mate. This is because we do not meet our soul mates by accident. Our soul mates are brought into our lives so that we can both have the experiences we need to progress in this incarnation.

Ancient myths can teach us valuable truths that we would not understand in any other way. Throughout the East, where reincarnation is considered a basic fact of life, there are ancient writings telling us that the soul originally consisted of both the male and female principles. This divine energy is spread throughout the universe by a process of division. Groups of cells gather in different places, all waiting to be transformed into souls. The smaller the group, the closer the association that these cells have with each other. Later on, in human form, these souls instantly recognize each other again whenever they happen to meet. The other cells in the group that you belonged to are all your soul mates. There is an immediate attraction and recognition at a soul level whenever two soul mates meet.

In Nigeria it is believed that people can arrange to be reborn together in their next lives to enable them to do things together. If someone is reborn, but no longer wants to take part in the joint undertaking, he or she is punished by a peculiar form of mental disturbance, which can only be relieved by having the person freed from the agreement by a native doctor.[1]

When people think about soul mates they quite naturally think about a perfect romantic relationship between a man and a woman. However, there are many other types of soul mate relationships. You might have an extremely close friend who has been your best buddy since childhood. This is likely to be a soul mate relationship, even though it is not a romantic one. You might have a special relationship with someone at work that could well be a soul mate one.

People who have influenced and affected you in different ways in your past lifetimes may well be your soul mates in this lifetime. Although none of these might be romantic relationships, they will always be learning experiences for everyone involved.

If you were extremely good friends with someone in a past life, you will experience a close bond in this lifetime also, and will have the opportunity to expand and develop your friendship. Likewise, if you hated someone in a past lifetime, you will recognize this person and will have the opportunity to become friends, or perhaps see some of the good aspects about this person in this present lifetime. Both of these people may well be your soul mates.

You are not restricted to one soul mate in love relationships, either. Soul mates can enter your life and leave it again. Consequently, a soul mate relationship can end in divorce or death. If your soul mate relationship ended this way, you can still attract another soul mate relationship to you.

There are almost seven billion people in the world today. There are many, many opportunities for you to attract the right soul mate to you.

I have an elderly friend called Bill. He has been married three times and is convinced that all three of his marriages were to soul mates. He married first at the age of twenty. His wife had just turned seventeen.

"We were both far too young," he admits. "But we tried hard to make it work. Betsy taught me a great deal, and I'm sure she learned something from me. We had two children in three years, and when my wife got pregnant again, she decided that she'd had enough. We separated, got together again, separated, and got together again. I knew nothing about soul mates back then, but I was aware of some karmic thing that kept us together, even though all my instincts told me it was over. It was an unhappy marriage, really, but all the same I was devastated when we separated for the last time.

"I stayed single for several years after that. My second wife came into my life by magic. She was a magician's assistant, and when she came down into the audience to pick a volunteer she chose me. I've always said that she mesmerized me. We got married about a year later, and had a wonderful life together. All the usual ups and downs, of course. My job took me away for one week in every month, but each time I came back it was like a honeymoon. We had forty incredible years together.

"When she died four years ago, I never dreamed that I'd find anyone else. But two years later, I met Adele, and my life has been absolutely perfect. We are on the exact same wavelength. We read each other's minds—she's better at that than I am—and think exactly alike. I have learned from all my wives, and, yes, I'm convinced that each one of them was a soul mate who came into my life to teach me the things I needed to learn."

Bill is still good friends with his first wife. "I took her to the movies just last week," he told me. "We do that every now and again, as her husband doesn't enjoy the movies, and I do. Adele has her embroidery club meetings on a Thursday night, and that's when I take Betsy to the movies. It gives us a chance to catch up on our children and grandchildren. We can discuss anything. We usually have all the world's problems solved by the time I take her back home!"

Bill considers himself an extremely lucky man. However, there is much more to it than that. He has met at least three of his soul mates. Most people never meet one. Bill is obviously doing something right.

"All I do," he told me, "is send the message out. I think about the perfect woman and how much I would love and cherish her. I do this every chance I have. Sooner or later, we meet. That's all there is to it!"

Bill is creating an atmosphere of positive expectancy. He remains positive and confident that this special person will come into his life. And, as he says, "sooner or later" it happens. Bill is a naturally positive person, anyway. It took him several years to find his second soul mate, but he remained quietly positive that it would happen. Most people would have given up long before then, but Bill is aware that we attract to us what we think about.

It is also possible to have more than one soul mate at the same time. This was brought home to me in 1983. By that time I had regressed hundreds of people back to their past lives and felt that I knew everything there was to know about the subject. I now know that this usually marks the stage where my real learning is about to begin.

On this morning I had a woman named Shirley coming in for a past-life regression at 10 A.M. She had been referred to me by another client and sounded excited about the prospect of discovering one of her past lives when she made the booking. Just before she arrived, another woman called and booked a past-life regression in the afternoon.

Shirley was a bright, vivacious woman in her early thirties. She had been hypnotized some years earlier to help correct an eating disorder. Consequently, she had no fears about being hypnotized and went easily into trance.

Her regression was an interesting one. She recalled a life in nineteenth-century Italy. She was called Elisetta, and was the oldest child in a family of twelve who made a subsistence living on a small farm in northern Italy. At the age of twenty she fell in love with Luigi, the son of a neighboring farmer. She had always admired him, but he became a hero to her when he joined Garibaldi's band of freedom fighters. Unfortunately, Luigi already had a girl-friend. This was Carolina, who had been Elisetta's best friend since childhood.

Luigi was enjoying his moment of glory and was flattered by the attention of two beautiful women. He promised Elisetta that he had ended his relationship with Carolina. In fact, this was not true. Luigi was attempting to have an affair with both of them. This was impossible in a small village and when the girls found out, they had a fight in the town square. Afterwards, they forgave each other and both vowed never to see Luigi again.

Fortunately, Luigi had left the village by this time and life returned to normal. Some months later he returned and tried to establish a relationship with both girls, again promising them that he had no interest in their rival. Of course, it was impossible to keep this quiet and the childhood friends became rivals once again.

One day Carolina and Elisetta went on a picnic. Carolina passed her friend a glass of poisoned wine. Elisetta accidentally knocked it over before drinking it. Carolina picked up the earthenware carafe that had held the wine and struck Elisetta on the head with it, killing her instantly.

It was a fascinating story, but once Shirley had left my office I was too busy to think any more about it. That afternoon I had my second regression of the day. Cynthia was about the same age as Shirley. She was a stunningly attractive blonde with penetrating blue eyes. She told me that something had impelled her to call me that morning. Up until a few days before she had never thought about the possibility of reincarnation.

It took a while before she was relaxed enough to hypnotize, but again she entered the required state smoothly
and easily. As she told me of her previous lifetime in a
small village in northern Italy I experienced a strong
sense of déjà vu. From what she told me it was obvious
that she had been Carolina in this previous incarnation. I
confirmed this by asking her what her name was. I then
asked her to tell me about Elisetta.

"Elisetta!" The hate and venom in her voice told me
everything. In a deep voice, almost like a growl, Carolina
told me of her relationship with the girl next door. How
they had been best friends until they each fell in love
with Luigi.

"I had him first!" Carolina snarled. "He was mine!"

"What did you do?" I asked, even though I already
knew the answer.

"We fought over him. In the marketplace. I pulled out
hunks of her hair."

"And then he went away."

Carolina sighed heavily and grunted. "Elisetta and I
became friends again. It was just as if nothing had happened. Except I missed Luigi."

"What happened when he came back?"

"He came back to me. But then Elisetta got her hooks
into him again. She spread her legs and Luigi was weak."

"What did you do?"

"I thought and thought. I never let on that I knew what
was happening. I pretended that we were still friends.

Then I invited her on a picnic. I put poison in the wine. When we got to our favorite picnic place I poured her a glass. But the stupid bitch knocked it over. She could tell from the look in my eyes what I'd tried to do. She started to get up. I grabbed the bottle and I hit her over the head with it. I hit her again and again, until . . ."

Carolina began sobbing quietly. I told her to step back from the scene and look at it impartially, as if it was happening to someone else. When the crying ceased I asked her to carry on.

"I dragged her to a bluff and tossed her over. Then I went back home and told everyone about the awful accident. No one questioned it, but I could tell that everyone knew what I'd done. I went to church every day, but I couldn't get the look in Elisetta's eyes out of my mind. When Luigi made love to me, it wasn't the same. He smelled and his love making was rough and crude. I couldn't see what I'd ever seen in him."

Carolina paused and gently shook her head from side to side. I waited for a minute and asked her to continue.

"One day I woke up early and left home. It was winter. I didn't know where I was going. I climbed up the mountain, looking for a good place to do it. I was scared, but I was cold inside. Inside I was already dead, and I knew that I was going to hell."

Again Carolina paused. She was shivering, even though my room was warm.

"All right," I said after a minute had passed. "I want you to see yourself, without pain, and without emotion, in the last few minutes of this lifetime that we're now exploring."

"It's cold," Carolina said. "And I can't do it. I want to throw myself over the cliffs, but I can't do it. It's so cold and I'm so tired."

"All right," I said. "Now it is just a few moments after you experienced physical death. You can look down on your body. What do you see?"

"Snow. Snow everywhere. Soon it will cover up my body."

Carolina had been unable to commit suicide in the way she intended, but the freezing cold and the snow did the job for her.

When she returned to full conscious awareness, I questioned Cynthia on her regression, and asked her if she knew Elisetta or Luigi in this lifetime.

"I've never seen Elisetta, but Luigi is my fiancé. His name's Tom. We're getting married in a few months."

I had been thinking of introducing Cynthia to Shirley, but this made me change my mind. I did not like the thought that history might repeat itself, and that I could be the catalyst to start it off.

However, I should have known that if Shirley, Cynthia, and Tom had been together in a past lifetime, there had to be a reason for them all to be alive again and living in the same city today.

Whenever I do a past-life regression I ask my clients to call me back in a few days to tell me of any further information that has come to them. Usually, once the door to the past life has been opened, much more information about the previous incarnation returns, and I enjoy hearing about this.

Shirley was the first to phone me. "You know when you asked me if I knew Carolina or Luigi in this lifetime, I said 'no'. But I wasn't 100 percent certain about it. Now I know who Carolina was."

"You do? Who is she?"

"I don't know her name. But she's a tall blonde woman who works in the same building I do. I've travelled in the elevator with her several times, and always had the strange feeling that I somehow know her. I know I haven't, so I've never spoken to her." Shirley then told me about some more details that had come to light. She finished by asking me if she should introduce herself to the blonde lady.

Inwardly, I was dying for the two of them to meet, but I was worried about the possible ramifications. I suggested that Shirley think about it for a few days first.

The following morning Cynthia phoned. "You know, that session helped me enormously," she began. "All my life I've been jealous of everything. I've never wanted to share. Now I know what caused it, and I've changed. I'm still changing. Even Tom's noticed it. Last night we went to a party and he spent half an hour talking to a beautiful woman, and I wasn't at all jealous. Previously, I would have stormed up to him and dragged him away. Then we'd have fought about it afterwards."

"That's great," I said. "I find these regressions help virtually everyone."

"Oh," Cynthia said, almost as an aside. "I think I know who Elisetta is."

I laughed. "She knows you, too."

"It's strange. I've known her by sight for a long while. I always felt that I somehow knew her."

"She feels exactly the same."

Cynthia showed no surprise that I seemed to know who Elisetta was. "I'm going to speak to her today."

"Please let me know what happens."

Shirley and Cynthia had lunch together the following day. They discovered that although they had never met, that they had friends in common, and had even played hockey against each other when they were at school. They had an instant bond, as if they had actually known each other always, which, in reality, they had. Cynthia had no qualms about introducing Shirley to Tom. Again, there was an instant recognition and an empathy, as if they'd always known each other. However, this time the two women were not competing for the same man. Shirley was happily married, and was fascinated to meet Tom, but had no intention of repeating what had happened in her previous lifetime.

Tom refused to meet me. Both of the women wanted him to have a past-life regression, but he would not even consider the idea. He acknowledged the instant connection and bond between all three of them, but he had no desire to have a regression himself.

A couple of years later, Shirley came back to me and had another regression. Cynthia and Tom figured in it as her two brothers, but there was no love interest.

My first thought was of the incredible coincidence that I should have happened to regress two of the three people involved at all, let alone both on the same day. However, on thinking about it further, it seemed less surprising. Shirley's desire to explore her past lives was obviously sending energy out into the universe, and this was subconsciously picked up Cynthia. This probably explains why she phoned and made an appointment just an hour before Shirley was due to arrive.

The other thought that came to me was how inextricably linked these three people were. In effect, they were all soul mates to each other. Obviously, they had all come back to this world in the same place, and at the same time, to continue learning the lessons that involved them all.

I remained in contact with the two women for several years, but gradually we lost touch. About five years ago, Cynthia came to a talk I gave and I had a cup of coffee with her afterwards. Cynthia, Tom, and Shirley had become close friends, and for a short time owned and operated a business together. Cynthia and Tom were happily married. Shirley had married and divorced, but was now in a permanent relationship with someone else. They were all extremely happy and the two couples saw each other virtually every week.

There is also evidence that indicates that groups of people are reincarnated together for a variety of purposes. Dr. Arthur Guirdham, a British psychiatrist and author of fourteen books, gradually became convinced that he, along with a group of others, had all been reincarnated together on at least five occasions covering a period of two thousand years.[2]

Edgar Cayce believed that the people who were involved with the conquistador invasions in Mexico and Peru, under Hernando Cortés and Francisco Pizarro, were reincarnated in the twentieth century to expiate their sins in the Spanish Civil War.[3]

There is no need to panic or worry if it is taking you longer than you thought to find your soul mate. All you need do is be patient, and send the message out. You are connected to your soul mate by a form of magnetic attraction. Sooner or later your soul mate will arrive. Later in this book we will discuss some exercises to help strengthen your magnetic attraction. These exercises are designed to speed up the process of finding your soul mate, but, all the same, you still need to be ready yourself. If you feel that you are not ready to meet your soul mate yet, read through the exercises, but do not attempt them until you are certain that the time is right.

There are many, many soul mates out there waiting to meet you. Finding a soul mate is probably the most exciting and fulfilling thing it is possible to do. Overnight your life will change. It will seem as if you have been living your entire life in black and white. When you meet your soul mate, your life is suddenly full of glorious color. Another comparison is the famous quotation from the Bible: "For now we see through a glass, darkly; but then face to face" (1 Corinthians 13:12).

Twin Souls

As well as your soul mates, there is one twin soul searching for you. This twin soul is your other half, dating from when we were all whole. It is most unlikely that you will meet your twin soul in this incarnation. It appears that your twin soul comes into your life when you are both experiencing your final life on this earth plane. A twin soul relationship is an unbelievably perfect relationship on every level.

You and your twin soul will connect with each other on the physical, mental, emotional, spiritual, and soul levels. Most people connect with their partners on one level, and some have no connection at any level. Good relationships are forged if the partners meet on two levels. Imagine what it must be like to be connected with your partner on all five levels.

To be totally in tune with someone at every level is a joy that all of us will experience one day, even though that day might be many incarnations away. In the meantime, though, we can enjoy a rewarding, joyous, fulfilling relationship with one of our soul mates.

5

How to Attract a Soul Mate

*If there is anything better than to be loved,
it is loving.*

—Anonymous

WE HAVE already mentioned in general terms how to attract a soul mate to you. You need to prepare yourself physically, mentally, emotionally, and spiritually and then wait patiently, but expectantly. This last part causes problems for many people. Not only do you have to wait patiently, which is no mean task in itself, but you also have to remain constantly expectant. By doing this, you in effect turn yourself into a magnet that will attract your soul mate to you.

There are a number of things you can do while you wait. One of the most important of these is to let go of the past. Do the exercise in chapter 3 and release all the excess baggage that is holding you back. The sense of freedom you will experience after doing this is incredible. You may have to do this exercise a number of times to finally let go of everything that has outworn its use.

Write down a list of all the qualities your soul mate will have. Be as specific as you can. If you forget to put down the person's approximate age, for instance, you might attract a soul mate who is ninety years old. Picture your soul mate as clearly as you can in your mind, and write down all the attributes that you see. It can be a good idea to do this over a few days. Every time you think of something, add it to the list. By creating a list in this way, you are consciously deciding what qualities you desire in a soul mate, rather than drawing to you whatever your subconscious mind attracts. Carry this list with you everywhere you go, and read it whenever you have a spare moment.

When you go to bed at night, think about your soul mate as you drift off to sleep. Picture him or her in your mind's eye as clearly as you can. See yourself doing pleasant activities together. By doing this you will attract your soul mate to you while you sleep.

You may, in fact, make initial contact with each other through your dreams. When you finally meet, you may discover that you shared the exact same dreams.

Think about your soul mate in spare moments during the day, as well. All of this adds power that helps to encourage your soul mate to you. As you know, we are what we think, and we attract to us what we think about. By thinking about your soul mate several times a day, you are strengthening your personal magnetism, which sends out a message to your soul mate.

Remove anything from your home that relates to previous partners. These serve to repel new relationships. This is particularly important in the bedroom. You may not want to toss out photographs and other mementos, but they should be out of sight, if you want to attract a soul mate.[1]

Keep positive. This means that you need to remain confident that you will find your soul mate. It also means that you need to think positive thoughts about yourself. Whenever you find yourself thinking a negative thought about yourself, switch it around as quickly as you can and make it positive. Whenever you berate yourself about your weight, height, or lack of success in any area of your life, you are putting yourself down. You need to feel good about yourself to attract your soul mate.

You can also use self-hypnosis to send out a message to the universe that you are ready for your soul mate. Some people become worried when the word "hypnosis" is used. There is no need for this. Self-hypnosis is similar to meditation in that you are physically relaxed, but are also mentally aware at the whole time. In meditation your energies become diffused, but in hypnosis your mind becomes concentrated on whatever it is you are trying to achieve—in our case, attracting a soul mate.

Hypnosis is highly beneficial. Every single cell of your body relaxes, and this is not necessarily the case when you go to sleep at night. I am sure you have experienced the feeling of waking up in the morning and still feeling tired, even though you have slept for your normal length of time.

Choose a time when you are least likely to be interrupted. Disconnect the phone temporarily. Relax comfortably on a recliner-type chair or on the floor. Use a bed only if you are planning to go to sleep immediately afterwards. This is because you are likely to fall asleep while doing this exercise. This does not matter if you have recorded the script onto a cassette as your subconscious mind will still pick up the message. However, if you have memorized the key points and are saying them to yourself in your mind, you will not want to fall asleep halfway through the process as you will lose most of the benefit of doing it.

You will have to decide whose voice records the script. You may wish to use your own voice, or perhaps ask a friend to record it for you. I usually record my own scripts for myself, but many people have told me that they prefer listening to a tape read by someone of the opposite sex. If you have a friend record it for you, make sure that their voice is pleasing to your ears.

You may want to have some gentle New Age-type music playing in the background. Do this if it helps you to relax. Do not use music that contains the sounds of water, though, as it may create a need to visit the bathroom part of the way through the exercise.

You lose about one degree of body heat during hypnosis, so make sure the room you are in is reasonably warm. You may want to cover yourself with a blanket before starting.

Soul Mate Attraction Script

Take a nice deep breath in, close your eyes as you exhale and allow all of your muscles to relax. Take another deep breath in and, as you exhale, allow yourself to relax even more. Nothing need bother or disturb you as you relax more and more with each easy breath you take. Each breath you take sends you deeper and deeper into this pleasant state of total and complete relaxation. Take another deep breath now, and, as you exhale, let all your doubts and fears and worries fade away until they totally disappear. Nothing need disturb or bother you as you drift down into a state of total peace and tranquillity.

It's so easy and so pleasant to relax like this, enjoying the pleasant warmth and the relaxation in every part of your body. Every part of your body is becoming so loose and so, so relaxed.

Become aware of the muscles in your toes and feet and just let them relax. You might feel a slight tingling sensation as they let go. Every breath you take is making you more and more relaxed, and your toes and feet are now completely, totally relaxed.

Allow that pleasant relaxation to drift up through your body now. Feel the relaxation moving into your calves, over your knees and into your thighs. Just so, so peaceful and s-o-o-o relaxing. Allow the relaxation to drift up into your hips now and then up and into your stomach. The lower half of your body is so relaxed now, and it feels as if your legs would not respond even if you wanted them to.

Each breath is slow and languid and lazy as you continue to relax. The pleasant relaxation is drifting into your chest now, and up, up into your shoulders. Tension gathers across our shoulders and it's wonderful to feel all that tension being evaporated away by the wonderful relaxation. Allow the pleasant relaxation to drift down both arms to the tips of your fingers. Now your arms and legs feel totally relaxed. So, so peaceful, and so, so relaxed. It's so pleasant to relax like this, and every nerve, muscle, and fiber of your entire being is loving the feeling of total, complete relaxation.

Allow the relaxation to move up into your neck. Feel the muscles of your face relaxing, and then allow that pleasant relaxation to slowly drift right up to the top of your head. Allow your scalp muscles to relax. Relax the fine muscles around your eyes. These are the finest muscles in your whole body and it feels so good to have them totally relaxed. You are now enveloped in total, absolute, complete relaxation. It's like resting on a fluffy cloud, with nothing to disturb or bother you. Feel the wonderful relaxation throughout your entire body.

You are relaxing more and more with every breath you take, and it feels wonderful to be so relaxed, with nothing to distract or bother you. Visualize yourself, in your mind's eye now. Scan your body and see if any parts are not as relaxed as they should be. If there is any tension anywhere, simply focus on it and allow the feelings of relaxation to dissolve the tensions and strains until you feel absolutely, totally relaxed.

You have reached a pleasant, enjoyable level of relaxation that is so beneficial for you. But you can go even deeper into this pleasant relaxation.

Picture a staircase in your mind. It's not an ordinary staircase. It's the most beautiful staircase you have ever seen, and your feet sink deeply into the soft pile of the carpet as you stand at the top and look down at the beautiful scene below.

It's not a long staircase. Only ten steps. Ten steps that lead you down to your very own secret room. It is a beautiful room furnished with the most magnificent objects you have ever seen in your entire life. There are couches and chairs and sofas and tables and potted plants. On the walls are gorgeous portraits of people who seem vaguely familiar. There are landscapes and other paintings as well. You can hardly wait to get down that beautiful staircase, so that you can examine them more closely.

But this is a wonderful, special staircase. Every time you take a step you double your relaxation, so that by the time you reach your secret room you'll be so, so relaxed, totally, completely, loose, limp, and relaxed in every fiber of your being.

Place your hand on the handrail now and take the first step, doubling your relaxation as you do. Feel the wonderful, soft, thick pile of the carpet beneath your feet.

Number nine. One more step, again doubling your relaxation.

Eight. Relaxing more and more.

Seven. Drifting down still further with each step.

Six. So relaxed now, as you drift deeper and deeper into a state of total relaxation.

Five. Pause for a moment at this halfway mark. Feel the total peace and tranquillity in every cell of your body. Nothing can disturb this wonderful feeling of absolute, complete relaxation.

Four. Deeper and deeper into a state of total peace and complete relaxation.

Three, relax, two, relax, and one.

Step off into that wonderful room. Walk around and examine some of the beautiful objects in your special, secret room. Virtually everything of beauty that you've admired in the past seems to be gathered together and displayed in this wonderfully relaxing, special room.

Have a look at the pictures on the walls now. There are magnificent portraits and wonderful landscapes. Pause in front of one of the scenes that you particularly like. As you look at the beautiful picture it seems to expand to accommodate you, and now you are inside the beautiful landscape, walking around inside it as if it is the most natural thing in the world to be doing.

And, as you are enjoying the sensation of exploring this beautiful scene, you become aware that someone is holding you by the hand. You realize instantly that it is your soul mate. As you turn to smile at him or her you find yourself looking into the face of someone who you have known forever. The two of you have been together in countless previous lifetimes, and the recognition is powerful and immediate. The attraction is like a bolt of electricity. You have both waited so long for this moment.

The two of you fall into each other's arms and lie down together in the soft grass. It is a magical moment, one that you'll remember forever. You taste your soul mate's sweet lips. You smell the fragrance of the grass. You hear birds singing happily overhead. In the distance a cow moos its congratulations. Every part of your body seems alive, in a way that you've never experienced before, and your senses absorb every precious second.

It seems as if you have spent your whole life waiting for this moment, and you wish it could go on and on forever.

As you gaze into your soul mate's eyes, you know that this is the rebirth of something that will flower and blossom and develop and grow for the rest of your life.

And now, you and your soul mate slowly separate and stand up again. You feel his or her hand take yours and feel a wave of excitement run right through your body. You are thrilled that you have found your soul mate again, and know that you will be together again forever.

You and your soul mate walk hand-in-hand across the field, and now you are out of the picture and back in your special, secret room. You look longingly at the picture, but you feel happy because you know that you can enter this picture again any time you wish. You also know that every time you do this, your soul mate is getting closer and closer.

Enjoy the special sense of being in your own secret room for a moment. Savor the fact that you can return here any time you wish. You might want to sit down in one of the comfortable chairs, or perhaps you'd like to examine more of the beautiful objects around you. It is your room and you can do anything you want here. You are protected and safe in your own special room, and you are welcome to return as often as you wish.

Now it is time to let go of all this and return to the present. On the count of five, you'll find yourself back where you started, in a quiet, relaxed, peaceful state, with a total recall of everything that happened while you were in this pleasant state of self-hypnosis.

One, take a deep breath in and let that vital energy spread throughout your body.

Two, coming up a bit now. Feeling invigorated, refreshed and ready to return to your everyday life.

Three. Thoroughly revitalized.

Four. Full of energy, and . . .

Five. Eyes opening and wide awake.

Repeat this self-hypnosis exercise on a regular basis. You will find it a relaxing and enjoyable experience, but more importantly, it helps to send out the message that you are ready for your soul mate to arrive.

You may need to be patient. Soul mates meet when the moment is considered right for both people. You may feel that you are ready, but your soul mate may not have reached that stage yet. Remain calm and confident that he or she will arrive when the time is right. Carry on with your life in your usual manner. Remain alert to the possibility that your soul mate could arrive at any time, but also be aware that in the greater scheme of things it may not be meant for you just yet.

Even when you do meet, it might take time for you to recognize your soul mate. As you know, memories of previous lifetimes are usually forgotten. No matter how wonderful and passionate your previous lifetimes were with your soul mate, they are usually locked out of your conscious memory. Consequently, it is a common misconception that you will instantly recognize each other. It does happen, of course. When it does, it is usually felt at the heart level. There is a sudden feeling of knowing the other person intimately, as if you know absolutely everything there is to know about your newfound soul mate. More usually, though, the awareness gradually surfaces that you have found your soul mate. As you get to know each other, you will suddenly find that the touch of a hand, the expression of love and tenderness in your partner's face, or the pleasure of a kiss will awaken long-lost memories. Sometimes you will both realize at the same time that you are, in fact, soul mates. At other times, one person discovers the fact, and the other person gradually comes to the same conclusion.

The knowledge that you have found your soul mate is indescribable. The intensity of the love and other feelings that emerge, and the incredible assurance that you are together for eternity, will give you more happiness than you have ever known. It will give you a sense of purpose and the knowledge that, no matter how difficult things might be at times, you will always have each other.

6

Why Isn't It Perfect?

But love is blind, and lovers cannot see
The pretty follies that themselves commit.

—William Shakespeare, *The Merchant of Venice*, Act 2, Scene 6

THERE IS a common misconception that soul mate relationships should be perfect in every way. If that were the case, every soul mate relationship would last forever.

Soul mates meet to enable both people to grow and develop in different ways. Two soul mates may meet in this lifetime to continue lessons that were not fully learned last time. For example, one partner might desire to control the other. It is likely that in a previous lifetime this person had been controlled, and now has to learn the lesson from the opposite point of view.

We bring to our relationships all our hopes, fears, dreams, desires, and expectations. We also bring a variety of hang-ups, unresolved problems, and a tremendous amount of other baggage. If you are seeking perfection, you are bound to be disappointed. Your partner may have totally different expectations. He or she might want to live life in a casual, unplanned way, living life for the moment. You, on the other hand, might want everything organized and planned to the nth degree. Obviously, in a relationship of this sort, there will be problems that can be resolved only with love and goodwill on both sides.

Friends of mine run an engineering business together. They have been married for twenty-five years and have two adult children. They have a good relationship in every area of their lives, except when it comes to running the business. He will come up with an idea, and then immediately want to implement it, no matter what disruption it causes to the smooth operation of the business. It will seldom occur to him to discuss his latest ideas with his wife and equal partner in the business. She, on the other hand, likes to think her ideas through before acting on them. She will work out a plan of action, and then consult the members of the staff who are likely to be affected by it. She will think about the repercussions if the idea does not work as planned, and will arrange to implement the idea step-by-step. Unfortunately, she does not discuss her plans with her husband, as she has learned from long experience that he is likely to ridicule any business ideas she comes up with. Consequently, it seems to the staff of this business that the two owners are frequently working in opposing directions, and are more likely to destroy the business than encourage it to grow. So, although this couple is happily married, they have difficulties in communication when it comes to their business. They claim that they are working hard at the business to leave it as a legacy for their children. Their son worked in the business for two years, but left, as he found it far too stressful. He was constantly expected to side with either his mother or father and the situation became impossible. Obviously, there are major problems here, caused by their different approaches to problem-solving, and I hope that they manage to work them out.

Sometimes it is difficult to tell if the problems couples have are karmic in nature. If one person is tidy, and is living with someone who is the opposite, the problems they have are probably not karmic. However, if one partner is abusive, or codependent, or subconsciously considers that he or she is unworthy of love, you can guarantee that karmic factors are present.

There is also the problem of thinking we have found our soul mate, when in fact, we have not. We might meet someone, fall in love, and think that we have found our soul mate. We may have a great deal in common, and have similar aims and desires. At the beginning, everything seems perfect. However, over a period of time, everything falls apart and we realize that the other person was not our soul mate after all.

Of course, life is not necessarily easy, even when we are with our soul mate. Soul mate relationships take many forms and there are an unlimited number of lessons that may need to be learned. Soul mate relationships last as long as is necessary for the lesson to be learned. One man I spoke to could not believe that his soul mate had suddenly left him with no warning.

"We were together for seven years," he told me. "I thought we were perfect for each other. I was happy, but obviously she was not. Why didn't she tell me? I'm sure we could have worked something out."

Quite possibly they could have. But in this instance, his partner had learned the lessons she needed to learn, and would have wasted time if she had stayed in the relationship any longer than was necessary. Even the way she ended it, by suddenly leaving without saying a word, might well have been a karmic lesson for her partner.

Hopefully, he will learn from the experience and ultimately find himself another partner. Unfortunately, some people become so embittered by an experience of this sort that they avoid future relationships and end up lonely and full of pain. This is no solution, as any karmic lessons are being avoided. Naturally, they cannot be avoided forever and will have be learned at a later date.

Many soul mate relationships are brief because the two people cross paths only to enable a particular lesson to be learned. These are usually nonromantic relationships. Teacher-student or employer-employee relationships are good examples of these. Once the student or employee moves on the relationship usually ends. However, while it lasts both people can learn valuable lessons.

At one time I was keen on fishing for trout. At a fishing lodge I stayed in I met an elderly man from South Africa who had been introduced to the sport fifty years earlier. A man he met by chance at a bar talked to him about the pleasures of fishing and invited him to join him the following weekend. During those two days, he taught my friend the rudiments of the sport, and effectively changed his life. After that weekend he never saw the man again, but he was convinced that it had been a soul mate encounter.

Soul mate relationships between family members are usually longterm ones, but again that need not necessarily be the case. A woman who attended one of my workshops told us that she had had an incredible bond with her father. Unfortunately, he was killed in a car accident when she was only seven. However, he had appeared to her in a dream shortly afterwards and told her that he would always be close. This had eased her grieving and she still felt him around her whenever she needed him, even thirty years later.

A successful author I know left home at the age of fifteen and never returned. His father had verbally and physically abused him throughout his childhood, and his mother, whom he adored, was powerless to stop it. It took him many years to come to terms with what had happened. He now realizes that both he and his father were continuing something that had begun many lifetimes before. In this lifetime he was being forced to become independent, and to stand on his own two feet.

We come into this lifetime to do certain things and to learn certain lessons. In effect, we agree on what we have to do before we are incarnated. However, not everyone is happy with the decisions they have made once they are on this earthly plane.

At one time I made my living as a palmist and numerologist. One of my clients was a wealthy property developer who had made millions of dollars in just a few years. I was surprised to find that he had a Life Path number of seven. This means that his purpose in this lifetime is to grow in wisdom and knowledge, and to develop a strong faith or philosophy of life. I had expected his Life Path number to be an eight, as this is the number of material freedom.

When the stock market crash of 1987 occurred, my client lost virtually everything, and he has spent the intervening years struggling to regain his lost wealth. He is aware that that is not his purpose in life, but because he had the money before, he desperately wants it again.

If he achieves it, it will bring him little pleasure or satisfaction, as it is not what he is here to do. He is an interesting example as the universe took his money away from him, to help direct him in the right direction. So far, he has ignored this strong hint. One day, hopefully in this lifetime, he will realize that money is not what he is here to achieve. Interestingly enough, he is aware of what he should be doing, but is constantly fighting it.

My client's lessons are not related to soul mates, but I have seen a number of examples of soul mates who agreed on something before they were born, and then decided not to do it once they were in physical form.

One example concerned a group of three people: Tania, Susan, and Aaron. They were all the same age and had known each other since they were children. Aaron married Tania, but a few years later had an affair with Susan. Susan expected Aaron to leave his wife, as they had made a commitment to be together before they were born. However, when it came to the point of leaving, Aaron found he could not do it. Consequently, in this incarnation, Aaron and Susan will not be together, and the lesson that all three participants have come here to learn will have to wait for another lifetime.

Everything happens for a purpose, even though we may not understand what it is. If your perfect relationship ends for any reason, be aware that it has happened in this way for a purpose. Some years ago I met a woman who had been happily married for several years. One day the police arrived and arrested her husband for several rapes that had occurred in their area. This woman could not believe it at first, and had to sit through the trial to fully understand the terrible things her husband had done. Even with this knowledge, she found it hard to divorce him, as she still loved him deeply. It took her years of therapy and counseling before she was able to fully live life again. She has no idea what drove her husband to commit those terrible crimes, but now realizes that it was all part of a plan that she is unlikely to understand in this lifetime.

Why is love so mysterious, powerful, and overwhelming? Why do relationships that start off with unbelievable happiness often end up in painful, bitter divorces? Why do we sometimes discover that the person we thought we knew is virtually a stranger who we do not know at all? These questions are impossible to answer, but they go some way to explain why some people have completely given up on the idea of ever having a good relationship, feeling that it's just not worth the pain, struggle, and effort.

Yet we all need love. I counseled a concert violinist some years ago. He had a wife and two children, but seldom saw them for any length of time as he travelled the world performing. Every day, no matter where he was, he called home to tell his wife that he loved her. One day, when he was several thousand miles away from home, she told him that she had had enough. She was leaving him and hoped to find a partner who would spend time with her and the children.

The violinist was devastated. He was almost through a tour and could not go home. When he finally returned, it was just as his wife had said. She and the children had gone, and his home was simply a house.

Fortunately, this man had his music, and he tried to hide his pain with a relentless program of performing. For twelve months he performed as frequently as he could. It did not work. When he came to me, he was miserable and incredibly lonely.

"I have women throwing themselves at me everywhere I go," he told me. "But I don't want any of them. I used to be lonely on the road. That's why it was so wonderful to have a special person I could call every day, someone I loved and who loved me. I feel empty, and the pain is getting worse and worse every day. I can't live without love."

"How is your wife handling the situation?" I asked.

"I have no idea," he replied. "We talk to each other through our lawyers."

I regressed him back to a past life one hundred years ago. He was a conductor of a music hall orchestra. He hated this work as his dream was to conduct a symphony orchestra. He was married to the same woman, and they had several small children. They constantly travelled from small town to small town to make ends meet. He dreamed of the big break he felt he deserved, and his wife constantly moaned about their life together on the road. Two of the children died, and a few months later his wife suddenly became ill with pneumonia and also died. Not long after this, he had the opportunity to become conductor of a large orchestra, but could not take it, as it would have meant leaving his children in the care of strangers. He became increasingly resentful of his lot in life, started drinking heavily, and was killed in a barroom brawl.

He was in a state of shock when he came out of hypnosis.

"And I thought I was having problems in this lifetime!" he exclaimed. "I had the same wife," he continued. "Why did she marry me again after what I did to her last time around?"

"Because she loves you," I said.

He stared at me for thirty seconds and then burst into tears. It was the best thing he could have done. He had been holding in all his pain and hurt, and the regression allowed him to release some of it. By the end of the session he had decided to return home and have a serious heart-to-heart talk with his wife. He would tell her how much he loved her, and see what sort of compromises could be made to save the relationship. Maybe he could cut back on his touring, and find more recording work.

"Why did it take me so many lifetimes to see?" he asked me again and again.

Fortunately, there was a happy outcome. His wife still loved him, but felt that leaving him was the only way she could bring him to his senses. She was as delighted as he was to continue with the relationship, and it is now better than it ever was. He still travels, but does much of it during school vacations so the whole family can be with him. He now spends much of the year teaching gifted students at master classes, and has a lucrative recording contract.

These soul mates are happy again because they love each other, and are prepared to make adjustments to their lives for the sake of their relationship. They no longer expect everything to be perfect. During the time of their separation, he wanted to die as he felt incapable of living without love.

No relationship is perfect. However, I believe that most relationships can be made to work if both partners want it to, and the couple love and respect each other. You might want the relationship to last, and be prepared to do the necessary work. However, your partner might be wanting to leave, for any number of reasons. If he or she is determined to leave, and there is nothing you can do about it, it is better to allow the relationship to end.

You deserve a close, loving, satisfying, and supportive relationship. Everyone does. However, it is unrealistic to expect perfection. We all make mistakes and do things that we regret later on. This is all part of our growth and development, and hopefully we learn from these mistakes. You and your soul mate have already learned a great deal from each other over many lifetimes, but there is still much to be learned.

7

How to Recall Your Past Lives

The best way to suppose what may come, is to remember what is past.

—George Savile, Marquess of Halifax
(1633–1695)

$\mathcal{M}$Y INTEREST in soul mates increased dramatically when I discovered that many of the people who visited my hypnotherapy center for past-life regressions came largely to see if their current relationships had figured in their previous incarnations. Many people were simply curious, but for others it was a way of verifying that they had, in fact, found their soul mate.

I was curious about this to begin with. It seemed obvious that people would instinctively know when they met their soul mate. However, not all soul mate relationships start with an instant recognition. They frequently start with a healthy lust on both sides, but this is characteristic of many relationships, even one-night stands. Many soul mate relationships start quietly and gently, and gradually the two people fall in love. These people sometimes wonder if their relationship is a soul mate one, and have a past-life regression to see if they can find out.

I have to explain to these people that even if their partner does not appear in the past-life regression it is not proof that he or she is not their soul mate. Soul mates do not necessarily find themselves in every incarnation. This may be accidental or deliberate. Obviously, if someone gets regressed back to a celibate lifetime, perhaps as a nun or a monk, he or she is unlikely to have a romantic soul mate relationship in that particular incarnation. This is all part of the soul's evolution.

Sometimes people find their soul mate, but because of circumstances the relationship is unable to develop. This might be due to parental disapproval of the other person, or perhaps one or other of the parties are already married to someone else and do not want to end that relationship. I have no idea how many thousands of regressions I've done over the last twenty-five years, but the combinations of relationships that I have heard about seems unlimited.

It is common for families to be together in consecutive lifetimes. The relationships change from incarnation to incarnation, but are easily recognizable by the person being regressed. Families are also often found inside larger groups, of perhaps fifty people, where friendships have a chance to grow and develop over many lifetimes. Sometimes these larger groups can be extremely complex, with every variety of human experience being acted out in the relationships between the people concerned.

It is easy to regress yourself back to explore your own past lives. I have done it hundreds of times. As mentioned earlier, it is usually better to do the first one with a competent, professional hypnotherapist. However, not all hypnotherapists are interested in performing past-life regressions. In fact, some are opposed to the whole idea of taking people back to their past lives. Many years ago, I wrote a book for hypnotherapists on this subject, and received several letters from hypnotherapists saying that I should not be encouraging their colleagues to enter this field.[1] Consequently, make sure that the hypnotherapist you choose is experienced and interested in conducting past-life regressions. Choose your hypnotherapist carefully, and insist that the session is recorded so that you have a permanent record of it.

Once you have experienced your first past-life regression you will find it a simple matter to regress yourself whenever you wish.

Of course, it may not be possible or convenient for you to seek out a qualified hypnotherapist. In this case, you will have to regress yourself back to a past life. You can do this either on your own, or with someone who you trust. Ideally, this other person will be someone who is just as interested as you are in exploring his or her past lives. This person will be able to guide you through your past lives, and you will be able to do exactly the same with him or her. The most important requirement is that you both trust each other. It is not usually a good idea to be guided by your soul mate. This is because your soul mate might guide your regression in directions that are of interest to him or her, but these may not be places you are ready to visit yourself.

This is the negative aspect of being guided by someone else. You might want to spend extra time in a certain place, but be hurried away by your guide. Conversely, your guide might linger in areas that you would rather not visit at this time. You need someone who is sensitive, sympathetic, and without a vested interest in what you discover.

Fortunately, you can return to the present at any time by simply opening your eyes. While visiting a past life, you are still totally aware of your current life. It is, for instance, impossible to be trapped in a previous life. Even if your guide walked out of the room and never returned, you would simply open your eyes after a minute or two.

Also, if your guide wants to explore areas that are either of no interest to you, or are too personal, you can always speak and tell your guide to move on to another aspect of the incarnation. You can also tell your guide to slow down if he or she is moving too fast. You are still in control, even when someone else is guiding you.

I remember experimenting with the use of a guide many years ago. People usually relax more deeply when they are being guided through a relaxation exercise by someone else, than they do on their own. Consequently, I thought that my recall of past lives might be better if I had someone to guide and direct me. (In practice, this turned out not to be the case, but it was worth experimenting to find that out.) My guide had regressed me to a life in Roman Britain. My father was a Roman soldier, but my mother was a local woman. Consequently, I was not completely accepted by either side, and had a difficult life. During the regression, I vividly recalled a sexual encounter with a girl my own age. We were both extremely young and made love quickly and furtively beside a river. I enjoyed reliving the scene, but once it was over I wanted to explore more of this lifetime. However, my guide kept bringing me back to the river to relive the sexual scene again and again. I became angry with my guide and told him to direct me elsewhere. He did so for a few minutes, but then brought me back to the river. I simply ignored him for the rest of the regression and explored this lifetime in the way I always do on my own. This demonstrated to me that you are always in control, and can always overrule your guide if it is necessary to do so.

It is extremely important that your guide is the right person for the task, and will do it seriously, ethically, and responsibly.

You can have several guides if you wish. One becomes the principal guide and the others ask questions with the object of broadening the experience. I have not found sessions of this sort particularly helpful myself. A regression should be taken seriously, and often the event becomes a party when a number of people are involved. Consequently, the questions asked tend to be flippant and the experience is generally unsatisfactory.

If you have practiced the "how to attract a soul mate" exercise in chapter 5 you will find the initial stages of a regression easy to do. Many people find it easy to relax, but then find it takes several attempts before they can let themselves regress back to a past life. There are a number of reasons for this.

Fear of the unknown is the main one. This fear is understandable, but is not necessary. In all the thousands of past-life regressions I have conducted over the years, no one came to any harm. Everyone returned safely. Admittedly, some people experience unpleasant scenes in their past lives, and this can be disturbing. This possibility is minimized in what we are going to do, because the script specifically says that you will experience the past life almost as if it was on a television set, and was happening to someone else. Even if you do become totally involved emotionally, you can always return to your present life at any time by opening your eyes, or counting from one to five. People do not realize until they regress themselves, that they remain aware of both this current life they are living as well as the past life they are exploring. Consequently, you can return to their present life in a split second if you want to. As a result, it is perfectly safe, and you are in total control all of the time. However, if you have fears and worries about it, it is a good idea to experience your first past-life regression with the help of an experienced hypnotherapist.

Some people find it hard to let go and return to a past life. This can be related to subconscious fears, but sometimes happens with people who are eager and keen to explore their past lives. If you find that you can relax easily, but find it hard to completely let go and return to a previous life, temporarily forget your desire to explore a previous incarnation and use the state of self-hypnosis to implant positive suggestions in your mind. You might say something like this:

> I am a positive, worthwhile person. I deserve to reach my goals. One of my aims is to explore my own past lives. I have the ability to do this. I am confident that I will be successful in achieving this goal, and I ask for divine guidance and help to assist me in doing this.

Once you have done this, simply become aware of your own breathing for a few seconds, and then silently count up to five and open your eyes. Remain positive that you can return to explore your past lives, and try again in a day or two. In my experience, about half of the people who regress themselves to a previous life succeed on the first attempt. Another quarter would succeed on the second attempt, and the others vary enormously.

You are not a failure if you do not succeed on your first attempt. Everyone is different. Take whatever time is necessary, remain positive and confident that you will succeed, and ultimately you will.

Naturally, you need to choose a time when you are not likely to be disturbed. The room should be pleasantly warm and reasonably quiet. Sit or lie down in a comfortable chair. A recliner-type chair is perfect for this. As you lose a degree or two of body heat in self-hypnosis, you might want to cover yourself with a light blanket. You may choose to play some gentle new age music as background. If you do this, choose something that is not instantly recognizable. You want to regress to a past life, not hum along to a favorite piece of music. I personally prefer to do without any background music when conducting past-life regressions.

You might choose to record the following script and play it to yourself. If you are using a guide to help you, this person can read the script out loud. Alternatively, you might want to become familiar with it, and then say it silently to yourself. There are advantages and disadvantages with all methods.

There are two ways of using a guide. The guide can read the script, while you experience the regression, but do not speak. Alternatively, the guide can ask questions at each stage, which you will answer out loud. This enables the regression to be recorded and you will be able to listen to it as many times as you wish. You will remember the experience, so there is no need to record the session. However, a recording is helpful if you have any questions six or twelve months later. I have not included questions in the script, as the questions asked are determined by the situation the person being regressed finds him or herself in.

If you are doing the regression on your own, you are less likely to become distracted or fall asleep while listening to a tape and following the suggestions given. The disadvantage of listening to a tape is that the recorded voice might hurry you on to the next phase of the regression before you have completely examined the situation you are currently in. I prefer to listen to a tape, but will repeat the regression without it if there are incidents and situations that I want to explore in greater detail.

Finally, relax in your chair and follow along with the suggestions on the tape. There is no need to analyze the words, or even pay a great deal of attention. Simply relax and enjoy the experience.

Past-Life Regression Script

Take a nice deep breath in, and close your eyes as you exhale. Let all your muscles relax from the top of your head to the tips of your toes. Take another deep breath in, and, as you exhale, picture your muscles loose, slack and relaxed. In fact, each breath you take makes you more and more relaxed, more and more relaxed. It's so peaceful and warm and tranquil to relax so thoroughly, and to drift down deeper and deeper with every breath.

Any outside sounds you hear will send you even deeper into pleasant relaxation. You're feeling loose and pleasantly relaxed now. Simply allow yourself to relax even more as you drift down deeper and deeper and deeper.

Become aware of the muscles in your toes. Feel them relax as you focus your attention on them. Allow that pleasant relaxation to drift into your feet now, and allow the muscles in your feet to relax. Enjoy the pleasant sensation. All of your body is relaxed now, but your feet are totally loose and slack.

Allow that pleasant relaxation to drift slowly up each leg, relaxing each area as it slowly moves upwards. Allow the relaxation to drift into your ankles, your calves, your knees. Up into your thighs now, until both legs are completely loose and relaxed.

Relax the muscles in your buttocks now and then allow the relaxation to drift into your abdomen and stomach. Such a pleasant feeling to relax and let go with nothing to disturb or bother you. It's so easy to do, and so, so restful.

Let the relaxation drift upwards now, into your chest. Feel the muscles in your chest relax, and then let the relaxation drift into your shoulders. Feel all the stress and strain and tension in your shoulders disappear as the pleasant relaxation takes over.

Now let the wonderful feeling of relaxation drift down both arms to the tips of your fingers. Allow your fingers and hands and arms to relax as much as they possibly can.

Feel the relaxation drifting into your neck now. Allow this relaxation to flow up and into your face, right up to the top of your head. Feel the muscles in your scalp relax. Allow the muscles around your eyes to relax. Feel the sense of this wonderful relaxation throughout your body. You are totally enveloped in a peaceful state of total relaxation and you are relaxing more and more with every breath you take. Relaxing more and more with each easy breath you take.

Picture yourself now in a beautiful room. Look at the magnificent furnishings and feel the thick pile of the carpet beneath your feet. Some of your most cherished possessions are in this room and you are happy to see them there. Other items that you have admired in the past are here, too. Paintings, sculptures, interesting knickknacks, and other things that you enjoy looking at. It feels so restful to be in this room, surrounded by all this beauty. But you know that you can go even deeper, because, in the corner of the room is an elevator, and you know that it takes you into an even deeper state of total and complete relaxation.

As you look at the elevator, the doors open, and it sits there waiting for you to get in. You step forward, intrigued by the beauty and opulence of this amazing elevator. As you walk into the elevator, the texture of the luxurious carpet beneath your feet seems to drain out any remaining stress and tension from your body.

The doors close now and the elevator goes smoothly downwards. It pauses at every level, and you realize that each stop is actually a doorway into one of your many past lives. All you have to do is think that you'd like to get out at a certain spot and the elevator doors will open and allow you to return to one of your many past lives.

And now the doors open, and you walk confidently into a specific past life that has relevance and importance to you in this present incarnation. *(Pause for thirty seconds)*

Allow yourself to become familiar with the environment. Look around and see where you are. See if there is anyone else there with you. And then look at yourself. Notice what you are wearing. See if you are male or female. Walk through the scene, absorbing every bit of information that you can.

And now, on the count of three, we'll have you move backwards or forward in this lifetime to see exactly how you spent your time. You'll be working or doing whatever else it was that you did on a normal, typical day. One, two, three. And now you're there. Again, notice everything. See who is with you and what they are doing. Observe what you are doing. Feel how you felt about what you are doing. Is it mentally stimulating? Is it satisfying work? *(Pause)*

Now, we'll leave that scene and move on to another time in this lifetime that we're now exploring. We'll go to a special moment in this lifetime. This is the time when you first met the person you loved most in this lifetime. On the count of three you'll find yourself meeting this person for the first time. Number one, two, and three. You are now there. Look around and see what you can see. Experience the feelings and emotions. Hear what is going on. Immerse yourself in this memory. *(Pause)*

Good. And now we'll move on to a particular, happy time that you are experiencing with the person who you loved most in this lifetime. On the count of three you will find yourself in this happy situation with this special person. One, two, and three. See yourself and the person you love together. Experience what you are doing. Feel the love and other sensations that are part of this special moment. *(Pause)*

And now we'll move on to a special, intimate moment the two of you shared. A time when the love you felt for each other was expressed. One, two, and three, you are there. Experience the bliss and joy of this special moment.

And now, on the count of three, we'll move on to a typical family scene. It is early evening and you and the other family members are all together. One, two, and three. Look around and become familiar with your family in this lifetime. Observe where you are and what is going on. See what everyone is doing, and become aware of their interactions with each other. *(Pause)*

Now, again on the count of three, we'll move to a time when you are with close friends. One, two, and three. See what you are doing. Observe your friends and enjoy the feeling of casual intimacy that you experience when you are with your closest friends. *(Pause)*

We are going to move ahead now to your very last day in this incarnation. You will not have died, and you will observe the events of this final day in a detached, unemotional manner, just as if you are watching it happen to someone else on a television screen. One, two, and three.

Go through the events of this final day. See how old you are, notice who is with you, and recall every incident up until the moment of death. *(Pause)*

And now, it is just a few moments after you have experienced your death. You are in spirit now, and you can look down on your physical body and observe the scene. Notice how you feel, and became aware of any feelings you may experience about that past lifetime we have been looking at. *(Pause)*

Did you do everything you wanted to do? *(Pause)* Were you as successful as you would have wished? *(Pause)* Were you happy, and loved by others? *(Pause)*

Are their karmic factors from this lifetime that still need to be worked on in your current life? *(Pause)*

An now, on the count of five, you are going to return to the present. You are going to leave this lifetime behind, but now that the door has been opened you will recall more and more about this lifetime over the next few days. It will gradually become clearer and clearer in your mind. And, of course, you can return to this past life as many times as you wish to explore it further.

Gradually returning now on the count of five. One. Feeling relaxed and comfortable. Two. You will remember absolutely everything that occurred during this regression. Three. Feeling calm and relaxed. Nothing need disturb or bother you. Four. Feeling wonderful in every way. And five. Back in the present, feeling comfortable, safe and ready to carry on with your everyday life. *(Pause)*

Now, I'll ask you to return to full conscious awareness on the count of five. You'll open your eyes feeling refreshed, invigorated, and full of energy. One. Feeling wonderful. Two. Coming back now. Three. In total control, relaxed and happy. Four. Almost there, and five, eyes opening and feeling wonderful.

After returning from your past life, sit quietly for a while and think about what you have learned. You might be surprised at what you have discovered. You may consider yourself an upright and honest person in this lifetime, but find that you were a thief in your past life. You may have done things that you would not dream of doing in this lifetime. Of course, the opposite might be the case, also. Some people become concerned when they change sex in a past-life regression. I recall one man who immediately opened his eyes and came out from his regression the instant he discovered he was a woman. He related it to a latent fear of being homosexual. This is not the case, of course, as we all experience many lifetimes as the sex opposite to what we are now. Incidentally, if a change of sex is a problem, while you are descending in the elevator you can specifically desire to return to a lifetime when you were the same sex that you are now.

I find it interesting to experience life in as many different ways as possible, and a change of sex is just one of those. One of my own past-life regressions had me living as a stonemason in the fourteenth century. It is the only lifetime I have found where I made my living entirely from physical work, and I have returned to it on several occasions to experience it more fully. In most of my past lives I have been a teacher, researcher, writer, or musician. I have been all of these things in my current life, and find it interesting to follow the development of my various interests through many different lifetimes. However, the lifetime as a stonemason stands out as being something completely different, and I have not yet discovered why I appear to have had only one lifetime doing hard physical work.

You can use this script verbatim if you wish. You can also add to it or change it in any way to suit yourself. You may find that the relaxation portion is not long enough to allow you to become totally relaxed. Simply enlarge that section to make it the right length for you. With practice you will find that it takes less and less time to become relaxed enough. I can hypnotize myself in a matter of seconds, but sometimes spend several minutes gradually relaxing myself as it is extremely pleasant to gently unwind, relax and let all the cares of the day fall away.

You can also change the past-life portion of the script. You might want to explore your childhood and find out about your relationships with parents, siblings, and friends. You might want to recall times when you were successful and achieving. You might want to go through your life stage by stage, recalling all of the high and low points in detail. You might want to attend your own funeral and see what is written on the gravestone. This last can be extremely useful, as it will list your dates of birth and death.

It is highly likely that you will want to examine your soul mate relationships in great depth. When you recognize a soul mate during a regression. make the most of the opportunity and explore your relationship then as thoroughly as you can.

Of course, you can ask any questions of yourself that you desire. At the very least I want to know my name, sex, occupation, or way in which I spent my time, and see the person who I loved most in that lifetime. Ideally, I also want to know whereabouts in the world I am, the dates of my birth and death, my hobbies and interests, and anything at all that I can use to verify the experience afterwards. In some of my regressions the details have been incredible, but at other times I seem to receive only a vague picture of what occurred, with no details that I can check later. I also like to see if the interests I have in this lifetime are the same ones that I had in the lifetime that I'm exploring.

I find it fascinating that interests that were important in a past life, but are not currently being used, can be relearned almost instantly. I regressed one woman back to a lifetime in Georgian England. In that life she was accomplished at needlework, something she had never done in this lifetime. She broke her leg shortly after the regression and, partly because of her regression memories, took up needlework as something to do while she was recovering. The work she produced immediately attracted attention and everyone marveled at how good she was, even though she had never done it before. Of course, she had, but two hundred years earlier!

Sometimes, for the sake of variety, I change the method of locating a previous life. Instead of going down in an elevator, I picture myself walking along a long hallway with doors on both sides. Behind each door is a particular past life. I can open any door I wish and immediately return to that particular past life. Another method is to imagine yourself floating five hundred feet up into the air and then descend to earth again into another lifetime.[2]

No matter which method you prefer, you will find it a fascinating experience to explore your past lives.

Once you have experienced a few past-life regressions you will find it interesting to regress yourself back to shortly before you were born into this lifetime. You will find yourself in spirit shortly before you entered your current physical body. You can now ask your soul as many questions as you wish. You will probably find that your soul does not really want to come back into another body, as it is totally happy and contented in the spiritual dimension. After all, it is in its natural home. If you ask why it is returning, you are likely to hear that it needs to come back for spiritual and soul development. In fact, you will find that it will be reluctant to return but has volunteered to do so because it is looking for opportunities to progress. You can also ask why it has chosen your particular personality for this incarnation, and any other questions that intrigue you. This can be a highly valuable experience, and one that will help you with your own growth and development.

A Sample Regression

Catherine had come to me because she was searching for her soul mate. She had been divorced for about two years and felt ready for a new relationship. However, this time she wanted to make sure that she found the right partner.

Consequently, once she was sufficiently relaxed, I suggested that she go straight back to the most recent lifetime in which she and her soul mate had been together.

"I think I'm there. It's cold, and it's dark."

"Are you indoors or outdoors?"

"Outside. It's a storm. I'm sheltering under the oak tree. I can see the blackness of the barn from here."

"Do you live on a farm?"

"'Course I do. This is home."

"Are you male or female?"

"Female."

"And how old are you?" (Sometimes I give the suggestion that the person will find themselves at a certain age in the past life. It is sometimes easier to tell the person to move backwards or forwards in time to a certain age. I use either the age of twelve or twenty. Twelve, because the person will have had enough experience to speak about the past life, but is unlikely to yet be in an important relationship. Twenty, because the person will probably be inside a relationship, or will else be looking for one. Theoretically, of course, I could ask them to return to any age at all.)

"Sixteen. Well, almost."

"What is your name?"

"Maureen."

"Okay, Maureen. What are you doing out in the rain?"

"'Twas a storm coming. Father wanted the sheep brought in."

"Have you done that?"

"All 'cept one. Can't find her."

"Do you know where in the world you live?"

"'Course I do. Somerset."

"What year is it?"

"December. December 1861."

"Do you go to school?"

Maureen snorts, and then giggles. "School? Me?"

"Do you have brothers and sisters."

"Yeah. Bone idle, the lot of them. I'm the oldest. Seven of us. Almost killed Mother, every one of us. Didn't stop Father, though!"

"Let's move ahead now. Let's move forwards until you're twenty-one. Are you still living on the farm?"

"Yes." Maureen shook her head violently. "Can't leave now."

"Why not?"

"Mother's passed away. I'm the mother here now."

"Do you have a boyfriend?"

A sly expression crosses Maureen's face. "You been spying on me?"

"Of course not. I'm just curious."

"Well. Not really. I sometimes see Tom Bellowes down in the village. He's sweet on me."

"Have you ever been out with him?"

Maureen giggles and claps her hands together. "What would people say? No. Never been out with him."

"Do you talk with him? Down at the village?"

"I tries to, but he's shy. Goes bright red when he sees me."

"Is he a farmer?"

"Well, he works on his folks' farm. Does what his father tells him. He reads, though. Reads a lot. Too much, I reckon. It's not good for you, all that book learning. Not enough practical, that's what Father says."

"Does your father like him?"

Maureen shakes her head. "Reckons he's dim. Not the full shakes."

"Okay, let's move ahead again. This time we'll move forwards until you are together with the person you most loved in this lifetime. On the count of three, you'll be there. One, two, and three."

"Can't do that."

"Why not."

"She's dead. Mother's dead."

"Of course. I forgot. Let's move ahead to the most serious relationship you had with a man in this lifetime that we're exploring. One, two, and three. Can you see him?" (I only used the words "see him" because Catherine was a visual person. In regressions some people "see" everything, other "feel" or "sense" things, and others simply gain an "impression." My choice of words is determined by the person I am regressing.)

"I see him. Sitting by the fire. Reading a book."

"Oh. Is it Tom?"

"Aye. Tom Bellowes."

"How old are you now?"

"Thirty-three."

"How is your relationship with Tom coming on."

"'Coming on'? It hasn't moved in twenty years! He's the same old Tom. Nose in a book all the time."

"Can you read, Maureen?"

The sly look crossed her face again. "Who've you been talking to? Ignorant, am I?"

"No, no. Just curious."

"Killed the cat. Curiosity."

"Tell me about your relationship with Tom."

"Nothing to tell. We meet in the village. Talk a bit. That's it."

"How do you spend your time?"

"I'm a skivvy for everyone. I wash, I clean, I cook, I sew, then I do it all again. Some life, eh?"

It was obvious that this lifetime was not going to provide much in the way of useful information. I decided to take her to another lifetime, but suddenly thought it might be interesting for her to see the last day of her life in the incarnation we were looking at.

"On the count of three, you'll find yourself in the last day of this lifetime. You will not have died, and you will watch the scene dispassionately, as if you are watching a movie. One, two, and three. Where are you?"

"In the village. By the green. I can see the Maypole. It's a lovely day. I'm talking with Tom."

"Is it good to see him?"

"What do you think? 'Course it is. There's noise. I hear a wagon. And the horse. A big black horse, bucking and kicking and trying to get away, dragging the cart. People calling out. I try to get away. I'm too slow, I'm kicked. I fall to the ground. Tom's there. He cradles me in his arms. I stare at his face, and he's crying. He holds me close. I can smell his leather apron. He tells me he loves me. Always has. But it's too late. I'm outside now. I'm above my body, looking down. I'm dead."

"All right, it's just a few seconds after you've experienced death. You're now in spirit and you're looking down at the physical body you have just left. Can you see your body?"

"Yes. Everyone's gathered around. People running, lots of shouting. They're all crying. Tom's beside himself. I didn't know any of them cared."

"Are you aware of any karma from that lifetime that is still having an effect on your current life?"

"Oh, yes. I need to give more. I need to make more effort. If I want something, I have to make it happen."

"Would you like to return to the present, or go back to another lifetime?"

Catherine gave a long sigh, and for a moment I thought she would prefer to return to the present.

After a long pause, she said firmly, "Another lifetime."

"Okay, take a deep breath in, and let it out slowly. See yourself walking down a long hallway with doors on each side. I want you to walk down that hallway until you reach a special door. You'll suddenly have a feeling that if you open that door you'll immediately return to a past life that will be especially beneficial to you. Let me know when you reach that door."

About twenty seconds later, Catherine told me that she had found it.

"Good. Open the door and step inside." I paused for half a minute to allow Catherine to become familiar with the environment.

"Are you male or female?"

"Female." She giggled. "Definitely female."

"Are you inside or out?"

"Outside. By the swimming hole."

"Are you on your own?"

"I hope so. I'm naked. I've had a swim and am drying off in the sun. I feel so free and happy."

"How old are you?"

"Seventeen."

"What is your name?"

"Kathy. My real name is Kathleen, but no one calls me that."

"And where do you live, Kathy?"

"Near Omaha, Nebraska."

"Do you know the year?"

"1923." For some reason, I had expected her to regress to an earlier life than the first one, and was surprised to hear the year. I questioned it, and she gave me the full date: July 21, 1923.

"Do you have a boyfriend, Kathy?"

"Sure do. His name is Will. We've been sweet on each other for three years."

"Good. I'll have you move ahead to a time when the two of you are together."

"I'm there. We're sitting outside a store eating ice cream. He has his arm around me and he's making me laugh so hard I can hardly eat. It's melting all over my hand." Kathy giggles. "He's touching my breast. In public! Oh no, here comes Mom." Kathy paused for ten seconds. "She's not happy. I'm walking away with her and Will's making faces at her behind her back. I'm trying not to laugh."

"Let's move ahead one year. Are you and Will still together?"

"Of course. I'm working in the insurance office and he comes in almost every day. We usually have lunch together."

"Does he come and see you in the evenings?"

Kathy shook her head. "No. Mom doesn't approve of him. She says he's fast."

"And is he?"

Kathy smirks. "I guess so."

"Okay. We'll move forward about three years. One, two, and three, you're there. How old are you now?"

"Twenty-three."

"Are you and Will still together?"

Kathy starts to cry. "We were, but he's gone away."

"Where is he now?"

"I don't know. It's my fault."

"What happened?"

Kathy starts sobbing. "It's okay, Kathy. Detach yourself and see it as if it's on a television screen, happening to someone else." I pause, until she stops crying.

"You can tell me if you like," I continue. "Otherwise, we'll move forward a bit more."

"I'm pregnant."

"And Will's the father?"

"Of course. He's the only one. I told him, and he left town. I thought he loved me."

"I'm sure he did, Kathy. Have you told your family?"

Kathy shakes her head violently. "No. I can't do that. I'm going to kill myself. That'll solve all my problems." Kathy began taking deep breaths as if she was hyperventilating. I was about to intervene, when she suddenly relaxed and smiled. "It's over."

"What's over?"

"That life. I've passed over."

"Can you see the body you've just left?"

"I don't want to look."

"Okay. Tell me, is there any karma or anything else from that life that is having a bearing on this life?"

"I need to be more open. I thought I was free. I was a rebel in my mind, but actually I was timid and held back. Held back too much."

"Okay. On the count of three, you'll find yourself sitting peacefully on the recliner chair in my office. Your eyes will be closed and you'll be calm, relaxed, and full of energy. One, two, and three. Very good. And now, on the count of five you'll open your eyes, feeling wonderful. You'll also remember absolutely everything that happened during this session, and your recall of those past lives will increase, now that you've opened the doors to them. Coming back now. Number one, two, three, four, and five, wide awake."

Catherine was ecstatic when she opened her eyes.

"That was Marvyn!" she exclaimed. "It was Marvyn both times."

As she had not mentioned Marvyn's name until now, I asked her who he was.

"He was my great love at high school. Everyone thought we'd get married, but he went away to college and found someone else there. I don't know where he is now."

I explained to her that Marvyn was obviously her soul mate, as they had been together in at least two previous lifetimes. However, the relationship had not worked out on either of the previous occasions, and it appeared that the same thing had happened in this incarnation as well.

"You probably have several soul mates," I told her.

"Marvyn is one, but there will be many others. Marvyn was obviously here so that you could learn lessons from him, and he would have learned just as much from you. It is quite likely that you will not see him again in this lifetime."

I was wrong. Two weeks later, Catherine phoned to let me know that she had met Marvyn again. He had separated from his wife and had moved back to town. He called Catherine and they talked for hours. When they went out for dinner, it was as if they had never parted.

I have no idea if they will end up together. I hope they do. They are obviously soul mates, and I hope that this time everything will work out well for them.

In transcribing this regression I have eliminated much material that was irrelevant, and have included mainly information that came through about Catherine and her relationships with her soul mate.

Normally, I take people back to one previous life. However, in this instance, we covered the first lifetime in about ten minutes, and it made sense to look at least one more. It was fortunate I had a feeling that her death in that first life was important, as otherwise that incarnation would not have provided anything of value.

There is no reason why you cannot visit several past lives in a single session. However, I prefer to explore past lives in as much depth as possible, and this is not possible if you are constantly skipping from one lifetime to another.

8

Other Methods

Methods are the masters of masters.

—Charles-Maurice de Talleyrand
(1754–1838)

*I*N MY own experience I have found hypnotic regressions to be the easiest and most valuable method of learning about your past lives, especially if you are primarily concerned with learning about your soul mates. However, many other methods can be used.

Lucid Dreaming

A lucid dream is a dream that you direct yourself. You are aware that you are dreaming, but do not wake up. The easiest time to lucid dream is just before waking up in the morning. By that time, you will have had most of the sleep you require, and will be half-awake. At this time, think about your need to find your soul mate and allow yourself to partially drift back to sleep. Follow the dream wherever it takes you. Guide it, if necessary, so that it leads you to past-life experiences with your soul mate.

As you know, most dreams are full of incongruous and illogical elements. With a lucid dream you are able to direct it away from these aspects, and allow it to uncover aspects of your previous lifetimes. It takes a great deal of practice to become good at lucid dreaming, but it is worth persevering, as the information that comes through can be extremely helpful.

Another good time to lucid dream is when you are under stress or strain, or are physically exhausted. Lucid dreaming is usually easier to do when you are experiencing difficulties in your life. At one time, when we were having problems with one of our children, I experienced lucid dreams every night.[1] However, stress is not necessary. With practice you'll be able to lucid dream whenever you wish.

Dowsing

When people think of dowsing, they usually think of someone looking for water with a forked stick. However, dowsing can be done in many ways, and can be particularly useful in exploring soul mate relationships.

For this purpose, the best method is to use a pendulum. A pendulum is a small weight attached to a piece of thread, cord, or chain. You can buy pendulums at new age stores, but any small weight attached to a piece of string will do. The best weight is about three ounces. The slight movements of lighter weights are hard to read, and heavier weights can be tiring. The thread needs to be between three and six inches long.

Pendulums have been used to answer questions for thousands of years. Marcellinus, who was the pope from about 296 to 304 C.E., wrote that a form of pendulum was being used in the first century.[2] In his history of the Roman Empire, Marcellinus described how a priest used a ring suspended on a thread to determine the successor to Emperor Valens. The ring was suspended over a circular platter that contained the letters of the alphabet, and the pendulum swung to indicate the letters T, H, E, and O. This told the conspirators that Theodorus would be the next emperor. Emperor Valens heard of the plot and killed the people plotting against him. This included several people who had names beginning with "Theo." However, he overlooked a man called Theodosius, and he ultimately became emperor.

Hold the pendulum by the thread between your thumb and first finger, with the weight hanging down. You will find it easier to use if you rest your elbow on

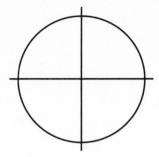

Figure 8.1 Pendulum chart

the table. I find it helpful to have a chart containing a circle, with two lines bisecting it (Figure 8.1, above).

Hold the pendulum over the middle of the chart. If it is moving, stop it with your free hand. When it is motionless, ask it which movement indicates "yes." You will find that your pendulum will start moving. It may move backwards and forwards, or from side to side. It may choose to go around in a circle, either clockwise or counterclockwise. If you have never used a pendulum before, it might take a minute or two to start moving. Remain patient, and it will answer.

Once you have a "yes" direction indicated, stop the pendulum and ask for a "no" direction. For some purposes, you may want to also ask for an "I don't know" and "I don't want to answer" directions, but this is not necessary when dowsing for soul mates.

Once your pendulum is providing you with positive and negative answers, you can ask it any question you wish. You might wish to ask: "Have I met so-and-so in any of my past lives?" If the answer is positive, you can carry on asking as many questions as you wish.

A friend of mine has become fascinated with the pendulum and has explored many of his past lives with it. So far he has looked at twenty-nine previous lives. He has been a male nineteen times, and has been married to the same person he is married to now in seven previous lifetimes. He has also been married to several other people, one of them nine times, and another four. Consequently, he believes that he has at least three romantic soul mates, though only one has ever appeared in any particular lifetime. He also has a small group of people who are usually with him in each lifetime. For instance, his brother in this lifetime has always been present, and his parents have appeared in most of them. Naturally, the relationships have changed each time, but he has been able to determine their presence using his pendulum.

He has even been able to use the pendulum to determine his sex in each lifetime, his dates of birth and death, the countries and even towns he lived in, the number of children he had, his occupation, and a wide variety of other things. He knows that, on average, each life lasted forty-two years. In one lifetime he died at the age of eighteen months, but in another he lived to the age of ninety-three. He was killed by accidents on seven occasions, illness twelve times, in war three times, and he was murdered once.

To determine your dates of birth and death, you need to ask a series of questions. Start by asking if you experienced a lifetime in the twentieth century before the one you are now living. If the answer is "yes," you can then proceed to find the actual date. If the answer is negative, you then ask if you experienced a lifetime in the nineteenth century, eighteenth century, and so on, until you receive a positive response.

Let's assume that the pendulum says you had a lifetime in the nineteenth century. Now you ask, "Was I born between 1850 and 1899?"

Again, we'll assume the answer is positive. Ask: "Was I born between 1860 and 1899?"

You keep on going in this manner until you receive a negative answer. Let's assume that you received a negative answer about being born between 1870 and 1899. This means that you were born between 1860 and 1869. All you do now is ask if you were born in 1860, 1861, 1862, and so on until the pendulum says "yes."

Determining the country of birth is done in a similar manner. You might ask if you were born in America. If the answer is "yes," you ask if it was North or South America. Then ask about individual countries until you get a positive response.

If the pendulum said you were not born in America, you might ask if you were born in Europe, Africa, Asia, or Australasia. Again, once you have determined the approximate location, you need to ask about individual countries. My friend had one lifetime on the Seychelle Islands, and he was almost pulling his hair out by the time he finally asked about that particular location. Determining past lives with a pendulum is a slow, drawn-out process.

Once you have the country, you can pinpoint the exact location. If the country is large, you might start by asking if you lived in the northern or southern part. It can be helpful to look at maps of the period when determining the exact location. For instance, you can waste time by asking if you were born in towns that did not exist at the time of your incarnation.

My friend "map dowses" to determine the exact location. This is done by using a pen as well as the pendulum. The pendulum is held to one side of the map, while the pen is slowly moved over the map. When the pen is indicating the area where my friend was born, the pendulum will give a "yes" reading.[3]

In my friend's case, determining occupations was an easy task. He has always enjoyed working outdoors, and in most of his past lives he has been either a farmer or a builder of some sort. His pendulum told him about a lifetime spent working on Salisbury Cathedral. As a result of that information, he visited Britain to see the cathedral. Once there, he recalled his past life, and he was able to pinpoint the places he had worked. In three lifetimes he was a monk or a priest. This surprised him, as he does not consider himself to be at all religious. However, I was not at all surprised as he has a great interest in Eastern religions and is searching for a purpose in life.

You may not find it as easy as he did to determine occupations. Start by asking about occupations relating to your interests in this lifetime, before asking about other types of careers. It is possible, but highly unlikely, for example, that you were a printer if you recall a lifetime in sixteenth-century Mongolia.

My friend has received a great deal of information from his pendulum, but unfortunately it cannot provide any of the colorful experiences and incidents that come out during a regression. Consequently, my friend uses a combination of both methods. He will determine, for instance, that he was born in 1512 in Antwerp. He was a banker, married twice, and had twelve children. With that information, he will regress himself back to that particular lifetime to explore it in greater detail.

I use the pendulum in the opposite way. I use it to clarify details that did not emerge during the regression. I might ask what the sexes of my children were, for instance. My friend has spent countless hours with his pendulum asking questions about his previous lifetimes. I prefer to experience them directly and use the pendulum only when necessary to provide greater insight.

Music

I have met several people who use baroque music to return to their past lives. Music by composers such as Albinoni, Bach, Corelli, Handel, Haydn, Mozart, Telemann, and Vivaldi are ideal. According to Mme. Belanger, a French researcher, the music of Mozart "coordinates breathing, cardiovascular rhythm and brain wave rhythm, and leads to positive effects on health. It acts on the unconscious, stimulating receptivity and perception."[4]

Not surprisingly, people listening to this type of music can involuntarily reach an altered state of awareness. Knowing this, many people have used this type of music to help them astral travel, learn more quickly and remember more, and to explore their past lives.

It is best to do this on your own in a reasonably warm room. You should wear comfortable clothes and relax in a recliner-type chair. Close your eyes and listen to the music. As you listen, you will find that your mind will wander. Whenever you become aware of this, tell yourself that you want to return to one of your past lives. You can be specific about the particular lifetime, if you wish. As you tell yourself of your desire to return to a past life, you will probably start focusing on the music again.

After this has happened a number of times you will find that on one occasion, instead of returning to the music, you will find yourself in one of your previous lives. Explore this life for as long as you wish, using the same techniques as in a hypnotic regression, and then, when you are ready, simply return to the present. If the music is still playing, listen to it for a few minutes before opening your eyes.

This sounds like an easy way of returning to your past lives, and, for some people, it is. I find it difficult myself, as I love classical music, and almost always focus on the music, and forget about the past life I want to explore. However, I know several people who use no other method, as it works so well for them.

Meditation

Meditation is similar to hypnosis. The main difference is that, when you are hypnotized, your physical body is relaxed but you are mentally extremely aware and focused on a particular goal. This might be losing weight or stopping smoking, for instance. It might be returning to a past life. In meditation, you are also physically relaxed, but your mental energies are diffused.

Some people find that when they meditate they can drift off into a past lifetime. This happens spontaneously. If someone specifically wants to return to a past life, the meditation then becomes a method of self hypnosis. When Rudolf Steiner was asked why people do not usually remember their past lives, he replied: "The entrance to the path is opened by right meditation."[5]

Mirrors

I have already mentioned how some people have seen their soul mates while looking in a mirror. This is usually involuntary. The mirror method explained here is one I teach to help people make contact with their spirit guides.[6] However, it also an excellent way of recalling past lives.

You need a good quality mirror and a white candle. The mirror should be a reasonable size. The one I use is two feet high and one foot wide. Hang the mirror on the wall in a position where you are looking directly at the center of it when you are sitting down. Place a small, circular, self-adhesive label to the mirror, just above the center. Consequently, when you sit in your chair in front of the mirror you should be looking slightly upwards to see the label.

Light the candle and place it in front of the mirror on the left-hand side. When sitting down, you should be able to see both the candle and its reflection in the mirror.

Turn out the other lights in the room and sit down on your chair facing the mirror. Relax as much as you can and stare at the round label on the mirror. Your eyes will soon feel tired. When you reach this stage, keep on staring at the circle, but start thinking of your need to explore one of your past lives. If you are seeking your soul mate, specify a lifetime when the two of you were together.

You will find, quite suddenly, that scenes from this past lifetime are reenacted in the mirror. Keep focused on the circular label. This is not easy to do. The tendency is to start watching the scenes as they unfold. As soon as you do that, the pictures fade away and the mirror becomes a mirror once again.

Do not worry if this happens. Everyone experiences this, even people who use mirrors for this purpose on a regular basis. When this happens, do not repeat the exercise right away. You are almost certain to experience the same problems again. It is much better to repeat the exercise at about the same time on the following day.

It is important that you take care of this mirror. Keep it clean and dusted, and do not use it for mundane tasks, such as brushing your hair.

Mirrors have been used as special, magical devices for thousands of years. You can use them to gain skill in clairvoyance, to make contact with your spirit guides, and to conduct a variety of rituals for different purposes. It is not surprising that the magical words "Mirror, mirror on the wall" play such an important part in the story of Snow White.

Astrology

It is possible to use astrology to examine any past-life relationships you may have had with your partner by drawing up and examining the two natal charts. A natal chart is a map of the heavens at the moment you were born. If there is a connection between the Moon, Neptune, cusp of the Fourth House, South Node, Vertex, or Part of Karma in the two charts, there will be a karmic factor present that indicates a previous lifetime together.

Many famous love relationships have occurred when the woman's Part of Karma was conjunct to the man's Sun. Examples are Elizabeth Barrett Browning and Robert Browning, Jackie Kennedy and John F. Kennedy, the Duchess and Duke of Windsor, and Nell Gwyn and Charles II.[7]

Obviously, the two people involved would have to have their charts drawn up and interpreted by a good astrologer. This method gives no indication about the type of past lives the two people would have had together, but it is another method of confirming the validity and reality of the past lifetime.

Psychics, Mediums, and Channelers

There are a number of gifted people who can give you a reading and, in the process, provide you with details about your past lives. However, you need to choose the person carefully. I would never go to a psychic without having received a recommendation from someone else first. This is because I have experienced more than my share of bad readings over the years.

Readers are human, of course, and have good and bad days, just like everyone else. A reader may give your friend a wonderful reading, full of valuable insights and helpful suggestions. However, this same reader may not be able to give you the same quality of reading. This may be because there is simply no chemistry between the two of you, and the reader finds it hard to obtain any useful information. Perhaps the reader is having problems in his or her own life, and is not as receptive as usual. Maybe the reader is burned out by giving too many readings, and desperately needs a vacation. There could be any number of reasons why the reader is having difficulty.

Channeled information is also hard to quantify. You are limited by the quality of the entity on the other side. Again, you should be cautious.

Fortunately, you can check any information you receive by regressing yourself back to the period of time referred to and seeing what you find there. It can be helpful to have the insights of someone who is not personally involved in the incarnation, as this can make you aware of factors that you might have overlooked otherwise.

There are a small number of reincarnation specialists who can check the Akashic records for you. Again, be cautious, and seek a recommendation before making an appointment.

Automatic Writing

When I was seventeen I met a man who wrote a novel by automatic writing. He simply sat down with pen and paper, relaxed, and the words came without any conscious input on his part. The pen moved and wrote the words at amazing speed. I was startled to find that he was equally as adept with his left hand, even though he was right-handed. Normally, he found it hard to write anything with his left hand. A number of published books have been written entirely by automatic writing. Examples include *Raymond, or Life and Death* by Sir Oliver Lodge and *Private Dowding* by W. T. Poole.

Automatic writing can open doorways into your past lives, but you need to be patient. It takes time for most people to become expert. However, once they can do it, the words can flow incredibly quickly. The Reverend George Vale Owen (1869–1931) received words at an average rate of twenty-four a minute, four nights a week, for months on end.[8]

It is important that you are relaxed and comfortable when practicing automatic writing. Your writing arm should have a ninety-degree angle at the elbow, and the pen should be resting comfortably on a pad of paper. Simply relax and see what happens. Some people prefer to have their eyes closed. I sometimes do this at the start to help eliminate any distractions.

After a while, the pen will start to move. Resist the temptation to watch what is happening. Try to ignore the movements as much as possible. Most people start off by drawing circles and other shapes. Some are able to do automatic writing while watching television or engaging in conversation. A few fortunate people start out by writing words and sentences. Some people even write words in mirror-writing. It does not matter what is produced, as anything at all indicates a start.

Once you have become used to it, the words will flow quickly and effortlessly. You will be surprised by what you produce. You may well find beautiful poetry being transcribed through you. You may find that you have written down solutions to problems that have been bothering you. You may even write a novel.

For our purposes, once you sit down with pad and pen, relax, and think about your soul mate. You might be searching for your soul mate. If so, think about that. If you have already found your soul mate, but are seeking information about previous lives together, focus on that. You may find it takes several sessions for any valuable information to come through. I find it hard not to show interest in what I am writing when I am thinking about soul mates. As soon as I do that, the material stops coming through. It is important to be patient and let the information come when it is ready.

It is better to practice for short periods of time on a regular basis than to have one lengthy session every now and then. You will be in good company if you experiment with automatic writing. Alfred, Lord Tennyson, William Butler Yeats, and Gertrude Stein are just a few people who have used automatic writing.[9]

Déjà vu

Déjà vu is the experience that you have seen something or done something before when you know that that is not the case. This is a common phenomenon that has occurred at some time to virtually everyone. It can often be linked to something you have done in a past life.

In *Omens, Oghams and Oracles,* I recounted an experience I had when I was twenty years old and visited Glastonbury Abbey for the first time.[10] It was a cool autumn day, and there were few people visiting the abbey. I suddenly felt a sensation of warmth and the abbey appeared rebuilt. Everything was illuminated with a special radiance. I felt as if I belonged there, and was, in many ways, home. Three months later, I returned to the abbey, hoping to experience the same feelings. To my delight, and bewilderment, I experienced the identical sensations again. This was an example of a déjà vu experience that involuntarily took me back to a partial recall of a past life. I have experienced similar sensations in a number of places, but none as vividly as that first time in Glastonbury Abbey.

Next time you have a déjà vu experience, pause and see if you can enter into the moment. Usually, we are puzzled for a second or two and then forget all about it. Instead of doing this, pause and see what happens. A déjà vu experience is usually an excellent window into a past life. You may well be surprised at what comes into your mind when you do this. Unfortunately, déjà vu experiences happen at unexpected times, and we are not able to arrange them at our convenience. However, it might be worth returning to a place where you experienced this sensation in the past, and see if it reoccurs, as mine did.

Far Memory

This is an interesting technique that can be extremely revealing, even if you do not recover past-life memories. You need to sit down comfortably in a chair, with your eyes closed. Think of an important experience that happened recently. Once you have it clearly in your mind, think about it for a moment or two, and then recall an important experience that happened earlier in your life. Gradually go back through your life, until you are thinking about important experiences that occurred in your childhood. The next step is to see if you can go back even further and recall an important experience from a previous life. Once you have found it, think about it, and then go back another step.

Another way of doing this is to deliberately choose some important events that have happened to you in this lifetime before you start the exercise. When you are sitting down, with your eyes closed, think about these events and the occurrences that led to them. See how far back you can take the events that led to these experiences occurring. Again, some of these may take you back into a past life.

I have found people who have been able to go back several lifetimes using their far memory. I have tried this myself, with mixed success, but have always found the exercise extremely worthwhile, as in the process I have been able to reevaluate different events that have happened to me in this lifetime.

Other Methods

I have included these additional methods for the sake of completeness. As I'm sure you know by now, in practice I prefer to enter into a regression. However, it is worth experimenting with these methods. You may find that you prefer them to a regression. At the very least, they will provide you with additional confirmation of what you have learned in your regressions.

9

Famous and Almost Famous Soul Mates

*The supreme state of human love is . . .
the unity of one soul in two bodies.*

—Sri Aurobindo

ℋISTORY IS full of examples of famous couples
who were soul mates, even though they, themselves, may not have been completely aware of
this. Anthony and Cleopatra, Heloise and Peter
Abelard, the Duke and Duchess of Windsor,
Queen Victoria and Prince Albert, and Nell
Gwyn and Charles II are just a few of the better-
known examples. Although these relationships
were all different from each other, they were all
characterized by an incredible bond of love that

time and death could not sever. Anthony and Cleopatra died young. Heloise and Abelard were separated for many years. The Duke and Duchess of Windsor overcame enormous difficulties before they could marry. Queen Victoria mourned the death of Prince Albert for decades.

However, there are many more examples of less famous soul mates, and their stories provide intriguing insights into the nature of soul mate relationships.

Robert Browning and Elizabeth Barrett

The story of Robert Browning (1812–1889) and Elizabeth Barrett (1806–1861) is a fascinating one. They first met when he was thirty-three and she was thirty-nine. She was bedridden, looked older than her years, and was being looked after by her pious father who said lengthy prayers at her bedside every night and forbade her to ever marry. At the time they met, Elizabeth was a near-recluse, emotionally dependent on her father, and looked forward only to death. She and Browning corresponded for four months before he was able to visit her, as she was so concerned about the effect her appearance would have on him. The day after they finally met he wrote to her, hoping that he had not offended her or stayed too long. The next day he wrote again proclaiming his love.

The relationship gradually developed. Elizabeth felt totally unworthy of his attention and love. The daily exchange of letters were originally signed "Yours faithfully Robert Browning" and "Elizabeth B. Barrett," but gradually became more and more intimate. By August, Robert Browning was calling her "My own, dearest love." Towards the end of that month, she told him the sad story of the death of her brother by drowning. In his reply, Robert Browning wrote: "Let me say now—*this only once*—that I loved you from my soul, and gave you my life."[1]

The antagonism of Elizabeth's father forced them to elope. After their marriage, Elizabeth's father ceased communicating with her. They settled in Florence where they both became heavily involved with their writing and the local community. In 1849, their son, Robert Barrett Browning, the sculptor, was born. One year later, Elizabeth's most famous work, *Sonnets from the Portuguese,* was published. This collection of forty-four sonnets vividly expresses her love and devotion to Robert, and was written during their two-year courtship. However, she did not present them to him until three years after their marriage. "Little Portuguese" was Robert's pet name for her. Before they were married Elizabeth had written a poem called "Catarina to Camoens," which described the feelings of a dying girl, Catarina, for her absent lover, Camoens, a Portuguese poet. Robert always associated Elizabeth with Catarina, which is how she received her pet-name. *Sonnets from the Portuguese* includes her best-known poem:

> How do I love thee? Let me count the ways.
> I love thee to the depth and breadth and height

My soul can reach, when feeling out of sight
For the ends of Being and ideal Grace.
I love thee to the level of everyday's
Most quiet need, by sun and candle-light.
I love thee freely, as men strive for right;
I love thee purely, as they turn from praise.
I love thee with the passion put to use
In my old griefs, and with my childhood's faith.
I love thee with a love I seemed to lose
With my lost saints—I love thee with the breath,
Smiles, tears, of all my life!—and, if God choose,
I shall but love thee better after death.

Elizabeth died in 1861 and Robert returned to London, where he continued with his career as a poet and dramatist. He spent the last years of his life in Venice and died there in 1889. He is buried in Westminster Abbey.

Robert Browning never understood his wife's interest in Spiritualism but obviously was intrigued with the concept of reincarnation. In "One Word More," he wrote:

I shall never, in the years remaining,
Paint you pictures, no, nor carve you statues.
This of verse alone one life allows me;
Other heights in other lives, God willing.

In "Old Pictures in Florence," he takes this even further:

There's a fancy some lean to and others hate—
That, when this life is ended, begins

New work for the soul in another state,
    Where it strives and gets weary,
        loses and wins:
Where the strong and the weak,
        this world's congeries,
Repeat in large what they practised in small,
Through life after life in unlimited series;
    Only the scale's changed, that's all. . . .

The last three lines of "Prospice" (meaning "look forward"), a poem he wrote shortly after Elizabeth's death, is particularly revealing:

    There a light, then thy breast,
    O thou soul of my soul I shall clasp thee again,
    And with God be the rest!

The love affair between Robert and Elizabeth has sometimes almost overshadowed the quality of the poetry they produced. After Robert's death, two volumes of their letters to each other were published, showing the deep love each had for the other.[2] The famous play, *The Barretts of Wimpole Street* by Rudolf Besier, is just one of a number of works written about their relationship.

The immediate love bond between Robert and Elizabeth was one indication that they were soul mates, and also proves the old adage "love is blind." Why else would Robert, a handsome thirty-one year old man, with a wide circle of attractive women friends, instantly fall in love with a bed-ridden invalid, several years older than him, whose face was ravaged by pain and suffering? Elizabeth delayed their first meeting because of concern about the way she looked. However, Robert fell in love, not with the sad person he met, but with a subconscious realization of the strong bonds they had experienced over many previous incarnations.

The astrological charts of Robert Browning and Elizabeth Barrett also provides a strong indication that they were soul mates. They had major aspects that indicated love and friendship, but also many lesser indications, including Elizabeth Barrett's Part of Karma being conjunct to Robert Browning's Sun. The conjunction between the woman's Part of Karma and her partner's Sun is also present in the charts of Jackie Kennedy and John F. Kennedy, and the Duke and Duchess of Windsor.[3]

C. S. Lewis and Joy Davidman

C. S. (Clive Staples) Lewis (1898–1963), the celebrated author of more than forty religious books, such as *The Screwtape Letters* and the delightful *Chronicles of Narnia* series of books for children, seems an unlikely person to have had a soul mate. In 1953 he was a professor of Medieval and Renaissance English at Cambridge University when he met the Greshams, an American couple with two young sons. At this time, C. S. Lewis was leading an orderly, spartan, chaste life, and did not really believe that there was such a thing as love.

Shortly after this meeting, the Greshams divorced, and Mrs. Gresham, now calling herself Joy Davidman, became Lewis' secretary. They married in 1956, but this was purely a marriage of convenience to allow her to continue living in England. Shortly after this, Joy developed a terminal illness. This changed the nature of the relationship and they married again with the blessing of the Anglican church. Miraculously, Joy's illness went into remission. The couple enjoyed a wonderful two years together before her illness returned and she died in 1960. Lewis wrote a poignant account of his despair in *A Grief Observed* (1961). Their love affair later became a play called *Shadowlands*.

In the midst of his grief, Lewis described what Joy had meant to him: "She was my daughter and my mother, my pupil and my teacher, my subject and my sovereign; and always, holding all these in solution, my trusty comrade, friend, shipmate, fellow-soldier."[4] An indication that they were soul mates comes a couple of sentences later when he wrote: "If we had never fallen in love we should have none the less been always together."

Obviously, it is impossible to work out what karmic factors were at play in this relationship. C. S. Lewis was obviously a sympathetic, caring person. After the First World War he had become intimate with Mrs. J. K. Moore, the mother of a friend of his who had been killed during the war. He began living with her and her daughter while still an undergraduate at Oxford. Over time,

Mrs. Moore became more and more demanding and possessive, but Lewis continued to look after her until she died in 1951. Despite this powerful learning experience, C. S. Lewis was still prepared to marry his secretary to allow her to stay in Britain. True love blossomed only when she was diagnosed with a terminal illness. What an unbelievable tragedy for him to lose his soul mate after just a few years of happiness.

Katherine Mansfield and John Middleton Murry

Katherine Mansfield (1888–1923) and John Middleton Murry (1889–1957) were also soul mates for just a few years. Katherine Mansfield was born in Wellington, New Zealand, and was educated there and in England. In her teenage years she had had a number of tragic love affairs with both men and women. She married in 1909, but left her husband on their wedding day.

Two years later, she met John Middleton Murry, who was at that time editing magazines that she wrote for. They began living together in 1912, but it was a free and open relationship as neither of them believed in fidelity. In 1918, she obtained a divorce from her first husband and married Murry. Over the next few years her reputation as a short story writer increased, but her health, never good, was eroded by tuberculosis. She travelled throughout Europe seeking a warm climate. She died in 1923.

Murry married again in 1924. His second wife, Violet le Maistre, gave him a son and daughter. Like Katherine

Mansfield, she died of tuberculosis in 1931. John Middleton Murry's son, Colin, considered his father's second marriage to be "an illusion," as Murry saw her as a reincarnation of Katherine.[5] Murry married twice more. His third marriage was an unhappy one, but his final marriage (in 1954) was successful. The couple had been living together since 1941, but could not marry until his third wife had died.

It seems that both Katherine Mansfield and John Middleton Murry were both desperately seeking a soul mate, found each other for a tragically short time, during which they experienced whatever lessons they needed to learn in this incarnation, and then moved on. In retrospect it might seem that Katherine had the easier time, as she was able to learn and progress more quickly, while Murry obviously had more lessons to learn about relationships. However, that is an overly simplistic way of looking at their lives. Only they can really know the lessons they had to learn.

Dorothy Osborne and Sir William Temple

The courtship of Dorothy Osborne and Sir William Temple would be unknown today if it had not been for the remarkable series of letters that Dorothy wrote to him between 1652 and 1654. These letters remained in the Temple family until 1891, when most of them were sold to the British Museum. The letters were first published in 1888. An enlarged edition was published in

1903, and in 1928 the Oxford University Press published the definitive version.

Dorothy and William met in 1648 on the Isle of Wight. She was twenty-one and he was twenty. He was on his way to Paris, but went with Dorothy to Guernsey, where her father was lieutenant-governor. When his father heard about this, he ordered William to Paris, where he spent the following year. The lovers were reunited in London, but again William's father intervened. He felt that William was spending too much time with Dorothy and not enough time on building a career for himself. Consequently, he was sent back to Europe for another year.

While he was away, Dorothy's family tried to find a suitable husband for her. They wanted her to marry someone with greater prospects and more money than William. William's father felt exactly the same. He wanted his son to marry someone with more money than Dorothy. Despite the tension and uncertainty that this created, Dorothy's letters show a practical approach to the situation:

> I cannot promise that I shall be yours because I know not how far my misfortunes may reach, nor what punishments are reserved for my fault, but I dare almost promise you shall never receive the displeasures of seeing me another's.[6]

It appeared that the two would never be able to marry, and Dorothy wrote to William, offering to let him go. She was deeply religious and did not want his passion to destroy him:

> I tremble at the desperate things you say in your letter; for the love of God, consider seriously with yourself what can enter into comparison with the safety of your soul. Are a thousand women, or ten thousand worlds, worth it? No, you cannot have so little reason left as you pretend, nor so little religion. For God's sake let us not neglect what can only make us happy for a trifle. If God had seen it fit to have satisfied our desires we should have had them, and everything would not have conspired thus to cross them. Since He has decreed it otherwise we must submit, and not by striving make an innocent passion a sin, and show a childish stubbornness.[7]

Dorothy's father died in March 1654, and Dorothy immediately made her longtime unofficial engagement public. Dorothy fell ill with smallpox in November, but was well enough to marry on Christmas Day 1654. Dorothy had a simple recipe for a happy marriage: "If we are friends we must both obey and command alike."[8]

William had a long and successful career as a diplomat, and Dorothy was able to accompany him on many of his visits to the continent. William's greatest success was in arranging the marriage between the Prince of Orange and

Princess Mary, later to become king and queen of Great Britain. Dorothy and William mixed in the upper echelons of society, and became friends with royalty. Dorothy became a patroness of the arts. However, Dorothy always suspected that it was impossible to find permanent great happiness. The couple enjoyed a long and happy marriage, but all nine of their children died before them, seven in infancy, and one by suicide.

In 1688, Sir William Temple gave up public life and began a new career in literature. He ultimately achieved fame as an essayist. In his *Essay on Poetry* he wrote:

> When all is done, human life is, at the greatest and the best, like a froward child, that must be played with and humoured a little to keep it quiet till it falls asleep, and then the care is over.[9]

Dorothy died in 1695. William died four years later. Jonathan Swift, the famous satirist, knew her well as he had been Sir William Temple's secretary. He described her as "mild Dorothea, peaceful, wise and great."

Dorothy and William enjoyed a long and happy marriage. They had obviously already learned their lessons about love in previous incarnations, and were using this lifetime to grow in other ways. However, their happy marriage was not simply a gift. It had been earned through a number of earlier lifetimes together, during which they would have learned their required lessons slowly and painfully.

Paraire and Kuini

In New Zealand, the song "Pokarekare Ana" is just as famous as the national anthem. Most people simply consider it a beautiful Maori song. However, it has an interesting history.

In 1912, in a small settlement on the east coast of New Zealand, a young Maori couple fell deeply in love. Their names were Paraire and Kuini. The couple wanted to marry, but Kuini's family were strongly opposed to the match. They did not like or approve of Paraire and refused to let her have anything to do with them.

Paraire was desperate. He had to prove to Kuini's family that he would be a good husband and provider. He wrote a love letter to Kuini, vowing to love her forever. As this did not seem enough to impress her parents he turned the letter into a passionate, heartfelt song—"Pokarekare Ana." He then arranged to meet her family at a famous *marae* in Gisborne. A marae is a meeting place where important discussions are held.

It must have been a highly stressful situation for Paraire as he went to meet Kuini's family and the local Maori elders of the tribe. However, Paraire gave a passionate declaration of his love and won the family over. They gave their consent to the marriage, and Paraire and Kuini enjoyed a long and happy life together. They were blessed with eight children and many grandchildren.

Where did the song that so impressed Kuini's family come from? "Pokarekare Ana" is a beautiful, melodious song that was drawn from the very depths of Paraire's soul. It was written with the single purpose of winning over Kuini's family so that he could marry her. It showed enormous originality and creativity, but Paraire never demonstrated these qualities again after winning Kuini's hand.

Bentreshyt and Pharaoh Sety the First

This extraordinary story of a soul mate relationship that lasted 3,000 years has been the topic of countless magazine articles, and became internationally known when Jonathan Cott and Hanny El Zeini wrote their bestselling book *The Search for Omm Sety*.[10]

The final chapter of the story began on January 16, 1904, when Dorothy Eady was born in London. At the age of three she fell down a flight of steps and was pronounced dead. The doctor went to get a death certificate. When he returned an hour later, Dorothy was sitting up and playing a game on the bed. Shortly after this, Dorothy began having recurring dreams in which she saw a large building with columns, beside a beautiful garden. Often, during the day, her parents would find her crying for no apparent reason. When they asked what the problem was, Dorothy would reply, "I want to go home."

At the age of four, her family took her on an outing to the British Museum. When they reached the Egyptian galleries, Dorothy raced around the room kissing the feet of all the statues she could reach. When the family wanted to move on, Dorothy sat beside a mummy in a glass case and refused to move. The family left her there and returned thirty minutes later. Again, she refused to move, and her mother picked her up to carry her out. Dorothy immediately said, "Leave me . . . *these* are my people!"[11]

A few months later, Dorothy's father brought home part of an encyclopedia that contained photographs and drawings of ancient Egypt. Dorothy was fascinated with these, particularly a full-page photograph of the Rosetta Stone. She would study this photograph for hours, using a magnifying glass to see the hieroglyphics. When her mother commented that this was a language that Dorothy did not know, the small girl replied that she did know it, but had forgotten it.

When Dorothy was seven, her father brought home some magazines. One contained a photograph of the Temple of Sety the First in Upper Egypt. Dorothy ran to father exclaiming, "*This* is my home! *This* is where I used to live!" Needless to say, Dorothy's parents were disturbed and worried about their daughter. Their concern increased when Dorothy found a photograph of the mummy of Sety the First. She ran to her father again, telling him that she knew Sety the First and that he was a kind man. Dorothy's father had had enough. He yelled at his daughter that the man in the photograph had been dead for three thousand years and she could not possibly have known him. Also, he was probably not a nice man. Dorothy ran to her room in her tears, and slammed the door shut behind her.

As she grew older, Dorothy began taking days off school to visit the British Museum. She met Sir E. A. Wallis Budge, the celebrated author and keeper of Egyptian and Assyrian Antiquities, who taught her how to read hieroglyphics.

At the age of fourteen, Sety visited her for the first time. Dorothy was asleep, but woke up when she felt a weight on her chest. She was surprised, but overjoyed, and cried out. Her mother came rushing in to the room and Dorothy had to explain that she had had a nightmare. She could not explain how her brand-new nightdress had come to be torn.

At the age of twenty-nine Dorothy married a young Egyptian man who took her back to Cairo to live. Her husband had no idea at the time that he was competing with a long-dead pharaoh for his wife's love. At this time, Dorothy had just vague impressions about her past life with Sety, but shortly after she arrived in Egypt he began appearing on a regular basis. In her second year in Egypt, Dorothy began getting out of bed in the middle of the night and, without fully waking, transcribed the words that were dictated to her by a "gentleman" known as Hor-Ra. Over a period of two years a full account of her previous life emerged.

In this past life Dorothy was called Bentreshyt (which means "Harp-of-Joy"). She was the child of a vegetable-seller and a soldier who served at a barracks about one mile from Sety's temple. Her mother died when she was only two. Her father felt unable to look after her on his own and took her to the temple to be brought up as a priestess of Isis. At the age of twelve, she was asked if she wanted to remain in the temple or move out into the world and find herself a husband. Bentreshyt knew no other life than that of the temple. As she was happy there, she decided to stay. This meant that she had to pledge to remain a virgin as she, in effect, became temple property.

Two years later, Sety came to Abydos to see how work was progressing on his new temple. One day he was in the gardens and heard someone singing. It was Bentreshyt. He asked her to join him. He was obviously captivated by this beautiful, fourteen-year-old girl with blond hair and blue eyes. Her great-grandfather had come from the Greek islands, and Bentreshyt's fair complexion made her stand out from everyone else at the temple. Sety and Bentreshyt saw each other several times after that, and soon became lovers. This was an appalling sin as Bentreshyt was temple property and a virgin princess of Isis. To make matters worse, Bentreshyt became pregnant.

Sety had to leave Abydos to attend to some problems in Nubia. While he was away, Bentreshyt was interrogated and finally admitted that her lover was Sety. Her crime against Isis meant that death was the only possible penalty. However, this would have involved a trial and people would discover that Sety had violated a princess of Isis. To protect her lover, Betreshyt committed suicide. When Sety returned, he was devastated by the news, and vowed never to forget her.

After three years of marriage in this lifetime, Dorothy and her husband divorced. It was a relief for both, and it freed Dorothy to pursue her love and work on Egyptian antiquities. After much persuasion, the Antiquities Department finally transferred Dorothy to Abydos in the 1950s, and she spent the rest of her life in the place that she had always called "home." She became known as "Omm Sety," which means "Mother of Sety."

The intriguing aspect of Dorothy's life in Egypt is that Sety visited her regularly, sometimes on the astral plane, but also in the flesh. He was able to materialize in her home where they were able to make love. This side of their relationship ended when she was transferred to Abydos. Sety explained to her that once again she was becoming temple property, and that neither of them could afford to make the same mistake again. He told her that both of them were being tested and, if they were able to resist temptation, their sin would be forgiven and they could then be together for eternity. Although they were no longer able to make love together, the visits continued throughout Dorothy's life. She knew that few people would believe them, so confided in just a few people, and recorded her other life in her journal.

These are just a few examples of the countless stories that could be told of historical soul mate relationships. Most such relationships have, of course, been lost in the mists of time. Fortunately, more and more stories are being recorded. An excellent example is the case of Elizabeth and Pedro, who had been lovers many times over the centuries, and found each other again in this lifetime thanks to the help of their psychiatrist, Dr. Brian Weiss. *Only Love is Real,* his fascinating account of their story, was published in 1996.[12]

Of course, most soul mate relationships are never recorded. The people involved are usually aware that they are in a special type of relationship, which they may or may not describe as being a soul mate relationship.

Finding your soul mate is obviously an important part of the process. Keeping your soul mate is just as important, as we will discuss in the next chapter.

10

How to Keep Your Soul Mate

One word frees up of all the weight and pain of life: That word is love.

—Sophocles (496–406 B.C.E.)

I AM SELDOM surprised when someone tells me that they had a deep, loving relationship with their soul mate, but that the relationship did not last. As you know, many soul mate relationships are not intended to be permanent. These are usually relationships when two people work on a project, or pay off a karmic debt, together. Once the task has been completed there is no need for the relationship to continue. Consequently, although the two may remain friends, they will also tend to drift apart. The relationship will cease to be as intense as it was when they were working together.

However, a warm, loving, soul mate relationship is usually different and is intended to be permanent. Of course, this is not always the case. Valuable lessons are learned if the relationship ends tragically, as was the case with C. S. Lewis and his wife, Joy. Robert and Elizabeth Browning were slightly different. They had thirteen wonderful years together, and both had probably learned the lessons that each had to learn from the other. Consequently, Elizabeth's death, sad though it was, gave Robert the freedom to return to England and carry on his career at a higher level than before.

Just recently a man in his late thirties came to see me. He was depressed and had totally lost interest in life. He told me that he had been married to the most wonderful woman in the world, but after twelve years of marriage she had left him. There was no one else involved. The couple had simply drifted apart.

I asked him what he had done to try to prevent the breakup of their marriage.

"I was so busy at work," he told me. "And when I realized, it was too late."

The couple had not sat down and discussed the situation, nor had they had any counseling. They simply divided up their possessions and separated. It seemed that neither party had been prepared to do anything that might save the marriage.

"Why don't you call her and invite her out for dinner?" I suggested. "Start all over again."

He appeared to consider my suggestion for a few moments and then shook his head.

"No, it's over."

A few days later he called and told me that he had acted on my suggestion. They were going to see a movie and he hoped that they might have a discussion afterwards.

It is hard to understand how someone who had found his soul mate ("the most wonderful woman in the world") could let her slip out of his life so easily. Yet this sort of thing happens all the time.

Obviously, this couple had been having problems. Rather than confront them and try to find a solution, the husband had simply spent more and more time at work, and then wondered why the relationship ended.

Situations like this need not occur. There are many things that can be done to keep a relationship alive.

The most important thing is love. As long as love is present, the relationship can survive and continue to grow. If the love has died, it is better to end the relationship as quickly as possible. Consequently, it is important that you tell your partner on a daily basis that you love him or her. There is no right time or place to do this. On the phone, or by e-mail, can be just as effective as saying it in person. Let your partner know how special you consider him or her to be. Express your love in different ways. Surprise your partner with an "I love you" card, or a bunch of flowers, for no reason at all.

It is natural for couples to take each other for granted as time goes by. Keep the romance alive in as many different ways as you can. One couple I know spend one night every month in a luxury hotel in the city where they live. They lead busy lives, and have no desire to travel. Ever since they got married, they have saved one night a month for each other and let nothing interfere with it.

This couple look forward to their one-night "honeymoon" every month. However, the romance can be kept alive in many other ways, small and large. An acquaintance of mine writes small poems to his wife telling her how much he loves and appreciates her. He happily admits that he is an awful poet, but his wife has kept and treasured every poem he has given her over the last twenty years.

A few years ago, a wise old man told me his favorite way to revitalize a relationship.

"Ask your partner what they would like to do for a weekend if they were given a certain number of dollars. Then, arrange it. Surprise your partner by giving him or her exactly what they asked for. Make sure that all of your partner's needs are attended to for this special weekend. Arrange a weekend that your partner will remember for the rest of his or her life."

Listening to each other is another vital component in a successful relationship. Problems occur when one person talks, but his or her partner does not listen. Often one partner talks more than the other. There are many reasons for this. The quieter partner may have trouble in expressing his or her innermost feelings, for instance. One person might naturally be quieter than the other. An imbalance like this does not matter, as long as each partner is prepared to listen, *really listen,* when the other person speaks. This is not easy. Most people are busy and our minds are full of everything that is going on in our lives. It is easy to drift off into a fantasy world when someone is talking to us.

I am particularly guilty of this whenever I am working on a book. When my children were younger they could always tell when I was writing a book as I would, quite unintentionally, go off into another world while we were enjoying a meal. They would speak to me and get no response as I was thinking about the book in my mind. Fortunately, it became a family joke, and hopefully I am getting better at listening and remaining in the present.

Neighbors of ours have an interesting exercise they do at least once a week. They devised it to improve open communication, but it is just as effective when done as a listening exercise. For three minutes, one of them would talk to the other. The listener was not allowed to interrupt or react in any way. The listener had to remain totally impassive and could not even nod his or her head in agreement. They used an egg timer to record the time. Usually the session begins with words such as, "I love you, but," and then the speaker has three minutes to say whatever is on his or her mind. Once the three minutes are up, the roles change and the listener becomes the speaker. They repeat this procedure as many times as are necessary to resolve any problems. It is a rule that each person has equal time. Consequently, the person who talks in the first three minutes has to be the listener in the final three minutes. This ensures equal time for each person.

When they first told me about this, I thought it was a terrible idea that could easily demolish a relationship. However, on trying it, I found the reverse is the case. Certainly, when you are the listener you hear things that you disagree with or are hurtful, but once it is your turn to speak these are forgotten as you say what is on your mind. Since learning this simple technique, I have suggested it to many couples. Without exception, they have benefited from doing it. The time period of three minutes can be lengthened or shortened. My neighbors used an egg timer as it made it easy to record three minutes. You might prefer one minute or ten minutes. It needs to be a length of time that suits both partners. In practice, I found it better to start with a short period of time and to gradually increase it as you both become familiar with the exercise.

What should you do if your relationship is in trouble? Every relationship has its ups and downs, of course. The important thing is to keep communicating with each other. However, many people find it hard to express their feelings. People like this are likely to bottle their pent-up feelings inside, and appear cold and indifferent. Inside they are hurting, of course. However, erecting a shield or barrier around themselves helps protect them from further pain. Be patient, if you are faced with this situation. Take your partner away from his or her familiar environment, and see if you can discuss the situation more easily elsewhere. No matter what your partner does or says, keep expressing your unconditional love for him or her.

You can also express your love to each other in prayer. You do not need to be religious to pray. Anyone can do it. Pray for your partner, and pray for your marriage. You can do this anywhere, at any time. You do not need to be inside a church or kneeling by your bed. You can pray while doing the dishes or driving to work. You can pray whenever you have a free moment. You might choose to say an affirmation prayer, such as: "Divine love is protecting my partner, myself, and our relationship." Alternatively, you might have a conversation in which you express all of your feelings and ask for help and guidance.

Henry Drummond called love "the supreme gift" and "the greatest thing in the world." Every word of his address *The Greatest Thing in the World* is worth reading over and over again, but there are two passages that are particularly relevant when discussing soul mates. They are:

> To love abundantly is to live abundantly, and to love forever is to live forever. Hence, eternal life is inextricably bound up with love. We want to live forever for the same reason that we want to live tomorrow. Why do you want to live tomorrow? It is because there is some one who loves you, and whom you want to see tomorrow, and be with, and love back. There is no other reason why we should live on than that we love and are beloved.[1]

> You will find as you look back upon your life that the moments that stand out, the moments when you have really lived, are the moments when you have done things in a spirit of love.[2]

Forgiveness plays an important part in long-lasting relationships. Everyone makes mistakes, and we all tend to blame others for our misfortunes. When we are feeling hurt and vulnerable we are inclined to lash out at whoever we think is responsible. Even the people we love the most. All this does is makes the situation worse.

When we forgive someone for what they have done, we are doing two important things. We are forgiving the other person, of course. More importantly, though, we are releasing all of the built-up negativity and resentment eating away at us like a disease. The sense of freedom that comes from forgiveness is incredible.

If two soul mates are having major problems in their relationship, it is highly likely that the initial problem began in a past life. Consequently, I suggest to these people that they find a competent person to regress them back to whatever incident it was that created the current problem. Once they understand the initial, instigating cause of their difficulties, the problem usually resolves itself.

One example I remember well concerns Duncan and Louise. I used to play tennis with Duncan when we were teenagers. I was pleasantly surprised to discover more than twenty years later that he was now married to an extremely attractive woman who had previously come to me for help in controlling stress. Much of her stress-related problems related to an overbearing, sexist boss who used sarcasm and ridicule to dominate his staff. Our hypnosis sessions enabled her to handle his abuse without suffering undue stress. I suggested that she change jobs, but she stayed where she was and now has her old boss' job.

When she called me some years after her initial sessions I assumed she was suffering from stress again. In a sense, she was. She and Duncan had been married for ten years and it was an ideal marriage in most respects. However, Duncan had strayed several times over the years and had brief relationships with other women. Whenever he was caught out, he would apologize and swear that it would never happen again. Of course, several months or a year later, it did. Louise had forgiven him in the past, but was getting tired of it. She was also finding herself doubting everything Duncan said. If he arrived home an hour later than usual, she would immediately think that he'd been with another woman. She wanted a past-life regression to see if she and Duncan had been together in the past. When they got married, she told me, she had been convinced that they were soul mates. Now she wasn't so sure.

At first glance it seemed that perhaps Duncan wanted sex more frequently than Louise, but apparently this was not the case. Louise told me that they both enjoyed making love, and she would initiate it just as often as he would.

She regressed back to a past life one hundred years ago in Upsalla, Sweden. She and Duncan were again married. Everything went well until Duncan arrived home drunk one night and tried to force himself upon her. She refused his advances. A fight ensued, which ended when she knocked him unconscious with a pottery urn. The next day, he moved out, but returned a week later. Although they remained husband and wife for another thirty years, he never made love to her again. He remained cooly distant and withdrawn. Periodically, Louise would hear rumors that her husband was visiting prostitutes, but the subject was never mentioned between them.

Louise was skeptical that this could be the cause of their current problems.

"I feel like hitting him on the head now," she said. "We have a good sex life. He doesn't need to go elsewhere."

Louise arranged for Duncan to come for a regression, also. This was the first time we had seen each other in twenty years, and he was reluctant about being regressed in case I heard information that was overly personal. I assured him that people can lie just as effectively while hypnotized, and that he would only ever tell me what he wanted me to know.

Usually, I try not to direct people to a specific lifetime, but in this instance it was important that we learned his views about his past life in Sweden.

It turned out that in this past life he was a quiet, deep-thinking man, with virtually no small talk and few friends. He was a heavy drinker, but seldom allowed himself to get drunk. He did not feel that he was totally intoxicated on the night when his wife refused his advances. He wanted to talk about it, but she refused. He remembered her picking up the urn and felt a sense of total disbelief as she swung it at him. It was pride that forced him out of the house the following morning, and it was lack of money that brought him back a week later. He felt unable to discuss the matter with his wife. Consequently, he retreated more and more into himself. Whenever he could afford it, he would visit a prostitute, but it gave him little satisfaction and simply increased his feelings of frustration about not being able to get close to his wife again.

Once he was back in the present again, I asked him if the experience had shed any light on their current problems. Duncan seemed dazed by the whole experience. The idea of reincarnation had never occurred to him, and he had visited me only to please his wife. He kept shaking his head in disbelief the whole time we discussed it.

"It's amazing," he told me. "We have a wonderful marriage, but every now and again I get this urge to have sex with other women. I've never known why, because we have a fabulous sex life. Yet, I jeopardize our relationship with stupid little flings, that don't mean anything.

"What Louise did to me in that past life was the right thing. I wouldn't want some drunk forcing sex on me. Maybe she shouldn't have knocked me unconscious, but she shouldn't have let me make love to her, either. I was too proud and too stubborn to ever discuss it with her. So I withdrew and punished myself and her. How stupid!"

"Do you think this might relate in any way to your present difficulties?"

Duncan pursed his lips. "Maybe. I don't know."

The following morning Louise called to tell me that they had had a serious discussion about their past life and the future of their relationship. No promises had been made on either side, but both felt as if they had made a major breakthrough.

I did not see them again for five years. My wife and I went to an outdoor music concert and they happened to be lying on the grass just a few yards from us. They had their arms around each other and looked extremely happy. Louise grinned at me and told me that all their problems were over. The trivial incident that had ruined their relationship in the past was not being allowed to do so again.

I was delighted to learn that the regression had solved their problems, and was happy that one session each was all that was required. Often several regressions are needed. This is because a karmic problem often extends over several lifetimes, and is not always resolved by looking at just one past lifetime.

None of us are going to lie on our deathbeds wishing that we had spent more time in the office or watching television. We are much more likely to spend those last moments thinking about the people we love, and who love us. What a tragedy, then, to let the special people in our lives slip away, when simple care, attention, and love could make all the difference.

Conclusion

Let those love now, who never loved before;
Let those who always loved, now love the
more.

> —Anonymous (translated from the
> Latin by Thomas Parnell, 1722)

ONE OF us should ever accept second-best in life. This applies to relationships, as well. Much of this lifetime will be wasted if you give up and marry someone who you know is not your soul mate. If you do this, you will miss out on, at least for this lifetime, the incredible love and passion that exists between two people who have been together in many, many previous lifetimes.

It might seem as if you'll never find your soul mate. There may be a lesson in this. Perhaps there are experiences you need to go through first. You may have to experience a difficult relationship first. Maybe you need to learn patience.

Remain confident that your soul mate is out there, and that he or she is also looking for you. When you finally meet, the period of waiting will seem like nothing. Remember, that even—and perhaps, especially—in a soul mate relationship, you must tend and nurture the relationship. You have had countless lifetimes together, and learned many things. The two of you have the potential to make enormous progress in this incarnation. Do not waste the opportunity by letting your soul mate slip away.

Did you know that scientists have discovered that falling in love usually involves a degree of mental illness? A team of Italian scientists, under the leadership of Dr. Donatella Marazziti, a psychiatrist at the University of Pisa, believe that this is the case. They have found that people suffering from obsessive compulsive disorders have about 40 percent less serotonin in their systems than normal people. People who are in love also have about 40 percent less serotonin in their systems.

They took blood samples from seventeen men and three women who were in love, and compared it to blood samples from twenty people suffering from the compulsive disorder, and twenty other people who were not in love and had no psychiatric problems. The volunteers who were in love or suffered from the disorder had 40 percent less serotonin than the other volunteers.

Interestingly, when the people who were in love were tested again twelve months later, after the first intensity of being in love had faded, their serotonin levels were back to normal.

Dr. Marazziti says: "It's often said that when you're in love, you're a little bit crazy. That may be true."[1]

Interestingly enough, William Shakespeare knew this some four hundred years ago. In Act Three, Scene 2 of Shakespeare's *As You Like It,* Rosalind says, "Love is merely a madness." Of course, Rosalind was madly in love with Orlando.

Find your soul mate and you can remain "a little bit crazy," and deeply in love forever.

Introduction

1. There are many translations of Plato's *Symposium.* My copy (translated by Seth Benardete) is included in *The Dialogues of Plato,* edited by Erich Segal (New York, N.Y., Bantam Books, 1986), pp. 251–254.

2. Gerald A. Larue, *Ancient Myth and Modern Life* (Long Beach, Calif.: Centerline Press, 1988), p. 155.

3. Barbara Watterson, *Ancient Egypt* (Stroud, UK: Sutton Publishing Limited, 1998), p. 32.

Chapter One

1. John Bradshaw, *Creating Love: The Next Great Stage of Growth* (New York, N.Y.: Bantam Books, 1992), p. 121.

2. William Faulkner, *Les Prix Nobel en 1950* (1951), p. 71.

3. Richard Webster, *Astral Travel for Beginners* (St. Paul, Minn.: Llewellyn Publications, 1998), pp. xi–xii.

4. C. G. Jung, *Memories, Dreams, Reflections* (London, UK: Collins and Routledge and Kegan Paul, 1963), p. 183.

5. Noel Street, *The Man Who Can Look Backward* (New York, N.Y.: Samuel Weiser, Inc., 1969), p. 43.

6. Although the concept of reincarnation is extremely old, the word "reincarnation" came into the English language just one hundred and fifty years ago. It is a compilation of five Latin words that mean "the process of coming into flesh again." (John Algeo, *Reincarnation Explored* (Wheaton, Ill.: The Theosophical Publishing House, 1987), pp. 133–134.) The word "transmigration" dates back to the sixteenth century and means "the transfer of a soul from one body to another." Other words with similar meanings are "metempsychosis" and "palingenesis."

7. George Gallup, Jr. and William Procter, *Adventures in Immortality* (New York, N.Y.: McGraw Hill, Inc., 1982), pp. 137–138.

8. Joe Fisher, *The Case for Reincarnation* (Toronto, Canada: Somerville House Publishing, 1998), pp. 5–6. (Originally published by Bantam Books, New York, in 1984.)

9. Dr. Ian Stevenson is the Carlson Professor of Psychiatry at the University of Virginia, and is also director of the Division of Personality Studies of the Department of Behavioral Medicine and Psychiatry. He describes his findings as "suggestive" of reincarnation, as obviously they can not prove the reality of reincarnation, even though they are extremely convincing. His most famous work is *Twenty Cases Suggestive of Reincarnation* (Charlottesville, Va.: University Press of Virginia, 1974). This book was first published as Volume 26, 1966, of the Proceedings of the American Society for Psychical Research.

10. Ian Currie, *You Cannot Die* (Shaftesbury, UK: Element Books Limited, 1995), p. 253. (First published in 1978 by Somerville House Printing Limited, Toronto, Canada.)

11. Helen Wambach, Ph.D., *Reliving Past Lives: The Evidence Under Hypnosis* (New York, N.Y.: Harper & Row, Publishers, Inc., 1978). (My edition was published by Hutchinson and Company [Publishers] Limited, London, UK, 1979), pp. 114–118.

12. Plato, *The Republic,* translated by A. D. Lindsay (London: Heron Books, 1969), p. 322.

13. Joe Fisher, *The Case for Reincarnation,* pp. 139–140.

14. The anathemas against Origen can be found in *A Select Library of Nicene and Post-Nicene Fathers of the Christian Church*, Volume 14, Series 2, edited by Henry R. Percival (New York, N.Y.: Charles Scribners Sons, 1900), pp. 318–320.

15. Geddes MacGregor, *Reincarnation in Christianity* (Wheaton, Ill.: Quest Books, 1978), p. 45.

16. Steven Rosen, *The Reincarnation Controversy* (Badger, Calif.: Torchlight Publishing, Inc., 1997), p. 72.

17. Hsueh Wen-yu, "'Fate' Brings People Together." Article in *Trademarks of the Chinese*, Volume II, edited by Chen Li-chu (Taipei, Taiwan: *Sinorama* magazine, 1994), p. 201.

18. *The Reincarnation Library*, Aeon Publishing Company, 540 West Boston Post Road, Mamaroneck, N.Y. 10543.

19. George du Maurier, *Peter Ibbetson*. Originally published as a serial in *Harper's Monthly* in 1891, and later that year in book form by Harper and Brothers, London.

20. Harry Leon Wilson, *Bunker Bean* (New York, N.Y.: The Curtis Publishing Company, 1912).

21. Gina Cerminara, *Many Lives, Many Loves* (New York, N.Y.: William Morrow and Company, Inc., 1963.) My edition is a Signet Book, published by New American Library, New York, in 1974, p. 99.

22. J. D. Salinger, *Nine Stories* (Boston, Mass.: Little, Brown and Company, Inc., 1948).

23. Plato, *The Republic*, pp. 312–316.

Chapter Two

1. Robert A. Baker, *They Call It Hypnosis* (Buffalo, N.Y.: Prometheus Books, 1990), p. 226.

2. Albert de Rochas, *Les Vies Successives* (Paris: Chacornac Frères, 1924).

3. Anonymous, *The Encyclopedia of Occult Sciences* (New York, N.Y.: Tudor Publishing Company, 1939), p. 464.

4. Robert A. Baker, *They Call It Hypnosis*, p. 227.

5. Joe Fisher, *The Case for Reincarnation*, p. 70.

6. Morey Bernstein, *The Search for Bridey Murphy* (New York, N.Y.: Doubleday & Company, Inc., 1956).

7. Morey Bernstein, *The Search for Bridey Murphy* (New York, N.Y.: Pocket Books, 1956).

8. Jeffrey Iverson, *More Lives Than One* (London, UK: Souvenir Press Limited, 1976).

9. The argument is still going on about the Bloxham tapes. One of the most vocal proponents of the negative point of view is Melvin Harris, a writer and broadcaster for the BBC. See *Investigating the Unexplained* by Melvin Harris (Buffalo, N.Y.: Prometheus Books, 1986). It is also worth reading *Mind Out of Time* by Ian Wilson (London, UK: Victor Gollancz, 1981).

10. Richard Webster, *Spirit Guides and Angel Guardians* (St. Paul, Minn.: Llewellyn Publications, 1998), pp. 275–278.

Chapter Three

1. Ralph Waldo Emerson, *Essays and Poems* (London: William Collins, 1954), p. 80. *Essays: First Series* was first published in 1841.

2. Ibid., p. 93.

Chapter Four

1. Joe Fisher, *The Case for Reincarnation,* p. 2.

2. All of Arthur Guirdham's books are worth reading. I particularly recommend: *The Cathars and Reincarnation* (London, UK: Neville Spearman Limited, 1970), *We Are One Another* (London, UK: Neville Spearman Limited, 1974), and *The Lake and the Castle* (London, UK: C. W. Daniel Limited, 1976).

3. Gina Cerminara, *The World Within* (New York, N.Y.: William Sloan Inc., 1957). My edition published in 1973 by C. W. Daniel Limited, London, p. 144.

Chapter Five

1. Richard Webster, *Feng Shui for Love and Romance* (St. Paul, Minn.: Llewellyn Publications, 1999), p. 95.

Chapter Seven

1. Richard Webster, *Cashing in on Past Lives* (Auckland, NZ: Brookfield Press, 1989).

2. This is similar to the method described by G. M. Glaskin in his book *Windows of the Mind: The Christos Experience* (London: Wildwood House, 1974). This book explains an excellent method of returning to a past life, but it requires two assistants as well as the person being regressed.

Chapter Eight

1. Richard Webster, *Astral Travel for Beginners*, p. 42.

2. Richard Webster, *Dowsing for Beginners* (St. Paul, Minn.: Llewellyn Publications, 1997), p. 57.

3. Richard Webster, *Dowsing for Beginners,* pp. 43–56.

4. Mme. Belanger, quoted in *Accelerated Learning* by Colin Rose (Aylesbury, UK: Accelerated Learning Systems Limited, 1985), p. 102.

5. Rudolf Steiner, quoted in *Masks of the Soul* by Benjamin Walker (Wellingborough, UK: The Aquarian Press, 1981), p. 91.

6. Richard Webster, *Spirit Guides and Angel Guardians*, pp. 200–202.

7. Rose Murray, *When Planets Promise Love* (St. Paul, Minn.: Llewellyn Publications, 1999), p. 145. (Originally published in 1995 as *When Will You Marry?*)

8. Terence Hines, *Pseudoscience and the Paranormal* (Buffalo, N.Y.: Prometheus Press, 1988), p. 25.

9. Richard Webster, *Spirit Guides and Angel Guardians,* pp. 175–182.

10. Richard Webster, *Omens, Oghams and Oracles*, (St. Paul, Minn.: Llewellyn Publications, 1995), pp. xi–xii.

Chapter Nine

1. Robert Browning, quoted in *Robert Browning: His Life and Work* by F. E. Halliday (London: Jupiter Books [London] Limited, 1975), p. 74.

2. *The Letters of Robert Browning and Elizabeth Barrett Browning*, two volumes, 1899.

3. Rose Murray, *When Planets Promise Love*, p. 145.

4. C. S. Lewis, *A Grief Observed* (Originally published by Faber and Faber Limited, London in 1961. The original edition was published under the pseudonym of N. W. Clerk.) My edition was published by HarperSanFrancisco in 1989, p. 60.

5. Harold Oxbury, *Great Britons: Twentieth Century Lives* (Oxford: Oxford University Press, 1985), p. 260.

6. Dorothy Osborne, *The Letters of Dorothy Osborne to Sir William Temple 1652–1654*, edited by Kingsley Hart (London: The Folio Society, 1968), p. 11.

7. Dorothy Osborne, *The Letters of Dorothy Osborne to Sir William Temple 1652–1654*, p. 144.

8. Dorothy Osborne, *The Letters of Dorothy Osborne to Sir William Temple 1652–1654*, p. 12.

9. Sir William Temple, *Miscellanea, the Second Part,* 1690.

10. Jonathan Cott in collaboration with Hanny El Zeini, *The Search for Omm Sety* (New York: Doubleday and Company, Inc., and London: Rider and Company Limited, 1987).

11. Jonathan Cott, *The Search for Omm Sety,* p. 13.

12. Brian L. Weiss, M.D., *Only Love Is Real* (New York, N.Y.: Warner Books, Inc., 1996).

Chapter Ten

1. Henry Drummond, *The Greatest Thing in the World,* 1883. There are many editions of this pamphlet. My edition is *The Greatest Thing in the World and 21 Other Addresses* (London: William Collins, 1964), p. 62.

2. Henry Drummond, *The Greatest Thing in the World and 21 Other Addresses,* p. 63.

Conclusion

1. Press Association article, "Madly in Love? You Said It . . . ," published in the *New Zealand Herald,* Section B, p. 1, July 30, 1999.

Suggested Reading

Bernstein, Morey. *The Search for Bridey Murphy*. New York, N.Y.: Doubleday and Company, Inc., 1956.

Bloxham, Dulcie. *Who Was Ann Ockenden?* London, UK: Neville Spearman Limited, 1958.

Bradshaw, John. *Creating Love: The Next Great Stage of Growth*. New York, N.Y.: Bantam Books, 1992.

Cannon, Dr. Alexander. *The Power Within*. London, UK: Rider and Company Limited, 1950.

Cerminara, Gina. *Many Lives, Many Loves.* New York, N.Y.: William Morrow and Co., Inc., 1963.

———. *Many Mansions.* New York, N.Y.: William Sloan Inc., 1956.

Currie, Ian. *You Cannot Die: The Incredible Findings of a Century of Research on Death.* Shaftesbury, UK: Element Books Limited, 1995. (First published in 1978 by Somerville House Printing, Toronto, Canada.)

Denning, Hazel M. *Life Without Guilt.* St. Paul, Minn.: Llewellyn Publications, 1998.

Dossey, Larry, M.D. *Recovering the Soul.* New York, N.Y.: Bantam Books, 1989.

du Maurier, George. *Peter Ibbetson.* London, UK: Harper and Brothers, 1891.

Fiore, Edith. *You Have Been Here Before.* London, UK: Sphere Books, 1980.

Fisher, Joe. *The Case for Reincarnation.* Toronto, Canada: Somerville House Publishing, 1998. (Originally published in 1985 by Granada Publishing, London, UK.)

Glaskin, G. M. *Windows of the Mind.* London, UK: Wildwood House, 1974.

Goldberg, Dr. Bruce. *Past Lives, Future Lives.* North Hollywood, Calif.: Newcastle Publishing Company, Inc., 1982.

Grant, Joan. *Far Memory.* New York, N.Y.: Harper and Company, 1956. Also published as *Time Out of Mind* by Arthur Barker Limited, London, 1956.

Guirdham, Arthur. *The Cathars and Reincarnation.* London, UK: Neville Spearman Limited, 1970.

———. *We Are One Another.* London, UK: Neville Spearman Limited, 1974.

———. *The Lake and the Castle.* London, UK: Neville Spearman Limited, 1976.

Hall, Judy. *Hands Across Time: The Soulmate Enigma.* Forres, Scotland: Findhorn Press, 1997.

Head, Joseph and S. L. Cranston (editors). *Reincarnation: An East-West Anthology.* Wheaton, Ill.: Quest Books, 1968. (Originally published by The Julian Press, Inc., 1961.)

Hodson, Geoffrey. *Reincarnation: Fact or Fallacy?* Wheaton, Ill.: Quest Books, 1967.

Holzer, Hans. *Born Again.* Garden City, N.Y.: Doubleday and Company, Inc., 1970

Iverson, Jeffrey. *More Lives Than One.* London, UK: Souvenir Press, 1976.

———. *In Search of the Dead.* London, UK: BBC Books, 1992.

Joudry, Patricia and Maurie Pressman. *Twin Souls: A Guide to Finding Your True Spiritual Partner.* New York, N.Y.: Carol Southern Books, 1995.

Jung, Carl. *Memories, Dreams, Reflections.* London, UK: Collins and Routledge, 1963.

Kingma, Daphne Rose. *Finding True Love.* Berkeley, Calif.: Conari Press, 1996.

Lancer, Bob. *The Soulmate Process*. Malibu, Calif.: Valley of the Sun Publishing, 1992.

MacGregor, Geddes. *Reincarnation in Christianity*. Wheaton, Ill.: Quest Books, 1978.

Mason, A. E. W. *The Three Gentlemen*. London, UK: Hodder and Stoughton, Limited, 1932.

Michael. *Finding Your Soul Mate*. York Beach, Maine: Samuel Weiser, Inc., 1992.

Moore, Thomas. *Care of the Soul*. New York, N.Y.: HarperCollins Publishers, 1992.

———. *Soul Mates*. New York, N.Y.: HarperCollins Publishers, 1994.

Moss, Peter and Joe Keeton. *Encounters with the Past*. London, UK: Sidgwick and Jackson Limited, 1979.

Murray, Rose. *When Planets Promise Love*. St. Paul, Minn.: Llewellyn Publications, 1999. (Originally published as *When Will You Marry*, 1995.)

Newton, Michael. *Journey of Souls*. St. Paul, Minn.: Llewellyn Publications, 1994.

Paulson, Genevieve Lewis and Stephen J. Paulson. *Reincarnation: Remembering Past Lives*. St. Paul, Minn.: Llewellyn Publications, 1997.

Perkins, James S. *Experiencing Reincarnation*. Wheaton, Ill.: The Theosophical Publishing House, 1977.

Ponder, Catherine. *The Prospering Power of Love*. Marina del Rey, Calif.: DeVorss and Company, 1983. (Originally published by Unity School of Christianity, 1966.)

Ryall, Edward W. *Second Time Round*. London, UK: Neville Spearman Limited, 1974.

Sardello, Robert. *Love and the Soul*. New York, N.Y.: HarperCollins Publishers, 1995.

Stearn, Jess. *Soul Mates*. New York, N.Y.: Bantam Books, 1984.

Stemman, Roy. *Reincarnation: Amazing True Cases from around the World*. London, UK: Judy Piatkus (Publishers) Limited, 1997.

Stevenson, Ian. *Twenty Cases Suggestive of Reincarnation*. Charlottesville, Va.: University Press of Virginia, Revised and enlarged edition, 1974. (Originally published as Vol. 26, 1966, of the Proceedings of the American Society for Psychical Research.)

———. *Cases of the Reincarnation Type. Volume 1: Ten Cases in India*. Charlottesville, Va.: University Press of Virginia, 1975.

———. *Cases of the Reincarnation Type. Volume 2: Ten Cases in Sri Lanka*. Charlottesville, Va.: University Press of Virginia, 1977.

———. *Cases of the Reincarnation Type. Volume 3: Twelve Cases in Lebanon and Turkey*. Charlottesville, Va.: University Press of Virginia, 1980.

———. *Cases of the Reincarnation Type. Volume 4: Twelve Cases in Thailand and Burma*. Charlottesville, Va.: University Press of Virginia, 1983.

Sutphen, Dick. *You Were Born Again to be Together*. New York, N.Y.: Pocket Books, 1976.

Todeschi, Kevin J. *Edgar Cayce on Soul Mates*. Virginia Beach, Va.: A.R.E. Press, 1999.

Ulrich, Thomas. *Made for One Another*. Woodside, Calif.: Bluestar Communications, 1998.

Underwood, Peter and Leonard Wilder. *Lives to Remember: A Casebook on Reincarnation*. London, UK: Robert Hales Limited, 1975.

Walker, Benjamin. *Masks of the Soul*. Wellingborough, UK: The Aquarian Press, 1981.

Walker, E. D. *Reincarnation: A Study of Forgotten Truth*. New Hyde Park, N.Y.: University Books, Inc., 1965. (Originally published in 1888.)

Wambach, Helen. *Reliving Past Lives: The Evidence Under Hypnosis*. New York, N.Y.: Harper & Row, Publishers, Inc., 1978.

———. *Life Before Life*. New York, N.Y.: Bantam Books, 1979.

Weiss, Brian L. *Only Love is Real*. New York, N.Y.: Warner Books, Inc., 1997.

Zukav, Gary. *The Seat of the Soul*. New York, N.Y.: Simon and Schuster, 1989.

Index

☽ REACH FOR THE MOON

Llewellyn publishes hundreds of books on your favorite subjects! To get these exciting books, including the ones on the following pages, check your local bookstore or order them directly from Llewellyn.

ORDER BY PHONE

- Call toll-free within the U.S. and Canada, 1-800-THE MOON
- In Minnesota, call (651) 291-1970
- We accept VISA, MasterCard, and American Express

ORDER BY MAIL

- Send the full price of your order (MN residents add 7% sales tax) in U.S. funds, plus postage & handling to:

  Llewellyn Worldwide
  P.O. Box 64383, Dept. 1-56718-789-7
  St. Paul, MN 55164–0383, U.S.A.

POSTAGE & HANDLING

(For the U.S., Canada, and Mexico)

- $4.00 for orders $15.00 and under
- $5.00 for orders over $15.00
- No charge for orders over $100.00

We ship UPS in the continental United States. We ship standard mail to P.O. boxes. Orders shipped to Alaska, Hawaii, The Virgin Islands, and Puerto Rico are sent first-class mail. Orders shipped to Canada and Mexico are sent surface mail.

International orders: Airmail—add freight equal to price of each book to the total price of order, plus $5.00 for each non-book item (audio tapes, etc.).

Surface mail—Add $1.00 per item.

Allow 2 weeks for delivery on all orders.
Postage and handling rates subject to change.

DISCOUNTS

We offer a 20% discount to group leaders or agents. You must order a minimum of 5 copies of the same book to get our special quantity price.

FREE CATALOG

Get a free copy of our color catalog, ***New Worlds of Mind and Spirit***. Subscribe for just $10.00 in the United States and Canada ($30.00 overseas, airmail). Many bookstores carry ***New Worlds***—ask for it!

Visit our website at www.llewellyn.com for more information.

Feng Shui
for Love & Romance

Richard Webster

For thousands of years, the Chinese have known that if they arrange their homes and possessions in the right way, they will attract positive energy into their life, including a life rich in love and friendship. Now you can take advantage of this ancient knowledge so you can attract the right partner to you; if you're currently in a relationship, you can strengthen the bond between you and your beloved.

It's amazingly simple and inexpensive. Want your partner to start listening to you? Display some yellow flowers in the Ken (communication) area of your home. Do you want to bring more friends of both sexes into your life? Place some green plants or candles in the Chien (friendship) area. Is your relationship good in most respects but lacking passion between the sheets? Be forewarned—once you activate this area with feng shui, you may have problems getting enough sleep at night!

1-56718-792-7, 192 pp., 5 ¼ x 8   **$9.95**

To order, call 1-800-THE MOON
Prices subject to change without notice

21 Ways to Attract Your Soulmate

Arian Sarris

Are you ready to meet your true love?

Do you desire to feel a deep, loving connection with someone? Do you want to find a relationship that works, one that makes you feel complete? Do you have the feeling that the right person for you is out there, somewhere?

You can't easily bring in your soulmate just by wishing. You need to light up like a Christmas tree, so the right one can't miss you! How you do that is the purpose of this book. First you will learn what a soulmate is, and the two kinds of soulmates. You will discover how to clear out the old to let in the new, and how to summon the help of your Higher Self and your angels. The book contains 21 exercises designed to help you dream your soulmate into reality, change the magnetic attraction of your aura, cut the cords of old relationships, create a soulmate talisman, and many more visualizations, affirmations, and spells.

1-56718-611-4, 264 pp., 5 ³/₁₆ x 6 $9.95